Amazon Nation
or Aryan Nation

White Women and the
Coming of Black Genocide

Bottomfish Blues

KER
SPL
EBE
DEB
2014

Amazon Nation or Aryan Nation
White Women And The Coming Of Black Genocide
Bottomfish Blues

ISBN: 978-1-894946-55-1

This edition copyright 2014 Kersplebedeb
first printing

Kersplebedeb Publishing and Distribution
CP 63560
CCCP Van Horne
Montreal, Quebec
Canada H3W 3H8

email: info@kersplebedeb.com
web: www.kersplebedeb.com
        www.leftwingbooks.net

"Freedom is the recognition of necessity."

CONTENTS

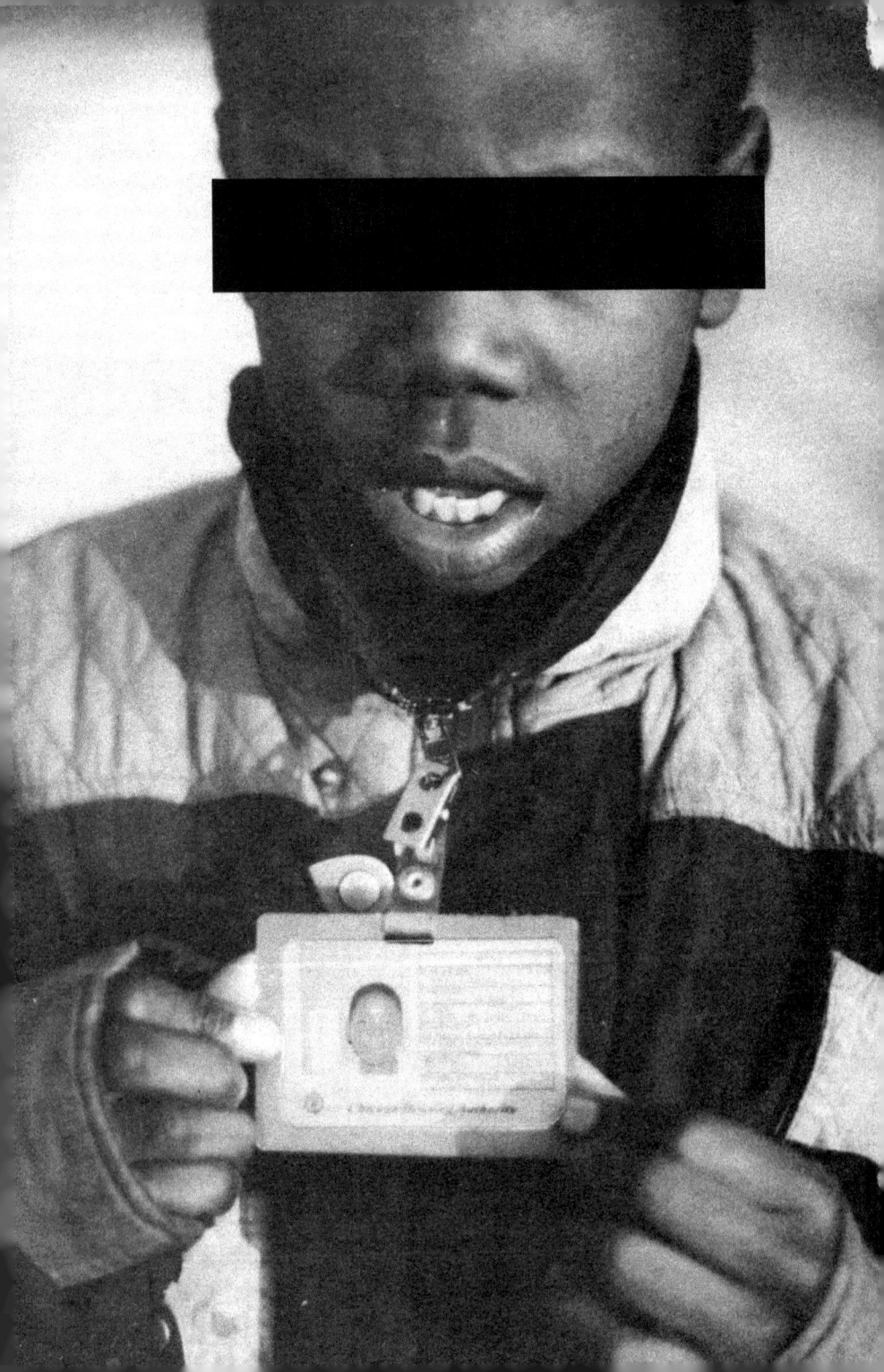

CRITICAL NOTE
TO READERS

THESE TWO AMAZON ESSAYS ARE NOT new but old, dating back to 1989 and 1990. *And in that lies their special value to us.*

These two writings were only fragments in a larger controversy, little noticed then. Coming to readers from an unexpected angle. From a larger political discussion in the new women's community of that time. As seen in an episodic and anonymous Amazon journal called *Bottomfish Blues* in 1989–1990. The unknown role of some radical euro-settler women in trying to sound the alarm.

The first article, "Kill the Kids First," is a long, bitter rant that factually traces what was happening at street level, in daily events, in New York City back then. This is important because New York was an early epicenter of the u.s. empire's new Black Genocide strategy. One breakthrough point where it became front page news, although in reverse form. It was a violent hurricane of imperialist hate institutionalized in state and business. In which a mob of thousands of euro-settler NY police could blockade their own City Hall, in one nighttime union contract protest that morphed into an undisguised hate rally. Newsmen on the scene watched a cop spitting on a New Afrikan city councilwoman trying to enter the building, as other cops nearby yelled "nigger whore" at her.

In the mornings, you walked the sidewalks in neo-colonial neighborhoods to the crunching of used plastic crack vials underfoot. Working-class New Afrikan women

were singled out for public abuse of all kinds, and increasingly denied employment or simply survival. As New Afrikan
housing was steadily wiped out block by block by fires and
bulldozers and settler gentrification. As long-established
communities "tipped" into depopulation.

All the destructive trends that are now being so anx-
iously talked about in the 21st century, were first surfaced in
New York City at that time. The mass incarceration of increasingly unemployed New Afrikan males, adult and child alike.
The "stop and frisk" apartheid policing that justified itself by
shrill alarms that any New Afrikans at all loose on the streets
was the priority public emergency. As the relentless emptying
out and gentrification of New Afrikan neighborhoods created mass homelessness (a recent 2013 study counted 22,000
homeless children in NYC). Entire communities started disappearing into New Afrikan dispersement and depopulation.
In fact, the homeless themselves were propagandized as the
new most dangerous criminal class. The center bulls-eye of
amerikkka's target.

Former and now reappointed NY Police Commissioner
William J. Bratton recently reminded euro-settler New
Yorkers of how their successful campaign to criminalize New
Afrikans started:

> *Many New Yorkers are too young to understand what the
> city looked like when I got here in 1990 – the graffiti, the
> decay, the crime, the social disorder. The police were not
> expected to do anything about these quality-of-life issues:
> aggressive begging, encampments in every park. When I
> came in as police commissioner, almost 300 people were
> living in the park across the street from the UN... To
> give you an idea of how things have changed, in 1990, I
> didn't go anywhere without a gun, because as the chief of
> the transit police, I did not feel secure anywhere, includ-
> ing in the subways...*

Commissioner Bratton really sums up amerikkka's genocidal settler spirit when he points out how the neo-colonies of homeless and unemployed justified him being personally armed (although he was also always accompanied back then by armed police bodyguards and still is). Of course, every day millions of women and children there used the subways and streets without guns. Just as Trayvon Martin used his streets.

Not everything the article analyzed necessarily proved out overall. Such as the authors' deep suspicions about the origins of the increasingly-New Afrikan AIDS plague. But twenty years later we pick these words up still bristling uncomfortably. With an array of disturbing insights about the murderous intentions of "post-civil rights America."

The second essay, "Integration," brings the focus down to euro-women's lives. It documents in detail one local political struggle in another city within the new women's community. Just women struggling with and against new awareness. As euro-settler women tried to work out and then had to fight out harshly between themselves what neo-colonialism was. In other words, finding that integration in the age of neo-colonialism equaled genocide.

So here is this buried intellectual explosive device, improvised and handmade by anonymous women in the previous generation. Remains of earlier battle, but still live and dangerous.

As an appendix, we have added a related but very different kind of article: *"The Ideas of Black Genocide in the Amerikkkan Mind."* It was written in 2009 by Butch Lee and J. Sakai, and was first passed around (although not published) as part of a collection of post-"Katrina" working papers on the New Afrikan crisis within the u.s. empire. We are using it because it gives readers some larger background of how Black

Genocide has always been present and publicly discussed throughout the u.s. empire's life. It is about how the "new normal" of euro-capitalism is always being violently engineered in blueprints of blood and cash.

KILL THE KIDS FIRST
THE COMING OF BLACK GENOCIDE

WHO'S BEEN SITTING IN DICK'S CHAIR, eating Dick's porridge, and sleeping in Dick's bed? We, that's who, doing it and liking it.

When we demanded to be let not only into Dick's house, but into his business and his government, and he welcomed us, we shoulda checked ourselves out. Really checked ourselves out.

Because Dick is carrying out Black Genocide, against the New Afrikan Nation and its communities. And we are right there beside him. Not an accident or an afterthought, but a carefully worked-out strategy to permanently answer the "Black Problem." Of course, we don't call it genocide or even racism when the white women's movement does it. We call it the struggle for equal rights or our equal privilege to swill at the trough.

We crave equality with Dick, which is the equality to oppress other people. We wanna gang up not get down.

Now, Dick don't care what we call it as long as we do "it". Early on Dick saw us coming. He read the cards, saw the plays and clearly understood what we still willfully fail to see.

White women's equality is the key to white solidarity that allows Dick to eradicate his lifelong dependence on Black labor and its dangerous potential.

Who'd ever believe that good old Jane would go along with this? In fact, white women don't believe that good father Dick, or son Dick, or brother Dick, or lover Dick are doing "it". We see what we wanna see. So we can do what we wanna do. But a careful examination of the facts of history and her-story tell a clear tale.

"Jane, Jane!" said Dick.

"Come and play.

I want to play something.

Will you play?"

Jane said, "I will play."

WHEN A MAN NEEDS A WOMAN

Today, two juggernauts are pushing their way into our common lives. They are the rising tide of genocidal violence against the Black community, and the unrestrained sexual violence against women.

Serial rape-murders, racial lynchings, child rape and the wholesale kidnapping of New Afrikan women and children from their communities, are becoming ordinary and everyday events in amerikkka. There is a unity in these events, a dialectical connection that meets in the strategy of genocide against New Afrika and the rise of the so-called women's movement.

Father & Son Inc. faces a problem. Go back to white amerikkka 1960–1970. You say you wanna kill 40 million Black people. You say your empire has to stamp out the flames set by 40 million New Afrikans imbeded in your Land base. You say you're engaged in a war ten million miles away in Vietnam. You say half your people are women who are imbed-ed in your homes, your offices, your factories, on their backs at the lowest level.

Women see the fires, smell the smoke, get the itch. They want up, you want them down but you can't turn your back. You need them more than they need you. You need white unity but on your basis. You hafta give up something. You can't afford to have white women on the other side. You need to replace the labor power of the New Afrikans you cannot trust in your cities. White women would be the perfect answer. They are more white than they are women.

But you need to police them. So with your dick in one hand and the civil rights act in the other, you offer "equal" rights if they walk your way and rape-death if they get loose. And along comes white Jane and says thanks. So let the show begin...

GENOCIDE HAS TO SNEAK UP

Genocide isn't new. Wasn't new with Nazi Germany. Wasn't new with the Indians. Genocide is old, a tried and trusted solution to the problem of intractable populations, people. Folks who get in the way and won't quit.

Things are known about genocide: the hows and whys. The technique and timing. We can't just get up one day and do it. We have to let it sneak up, look accidental, be acceptable, fade into everyday events. We have to say it is unthinkable, something only madmen do.

We can't admit that it is natural, intrinsic to your white, patriarchal imperial culture. If peoples saw it coming then it can't be done. It must seem like a series of small answers to things everyone agrees are problems. We can't just jump up and propose it on the 7 o'clock news.

So what do we tell a people when they begin to suspect that they are up against execution, mass death? What do we say about genocide when our intended victims begin to whisper the word?

Think about what amerikkka, the media and schools, really say about genocide. We say the Nazis slaughtered 6 million Jews in gas chambers and ovens. We say men did it back in the '40s with bullets and cyanide gas. We say it over and over. Genocide, we say, is something men did and women have nothing to do with it.

But when do we talk about the twenty years of preparation in Germany that led up to the death camps?

We never do, do we?

That is what i want to talk about. What the years of preparation look like from the inside. A report from amerikkka, where we're already dreaming about throwing a monster block party to celebrate Black disappearance day. It has already begun.

In the beginning are the kidnapped children. Close

down the future by starting to kidnap and kill off Black children. This is the Jefferson Plan, first proposed by u.s. president Thomas Jefferson. Who helped write the u.s. constitution and bill of rights. A slaveowner, Thomas Jefferson was worried that someday Afrikans might overthrow the white masters and take over the u.s. He wrote *"a revolution of the wheel of fortune, an exchange of situation is among possible events."*

His proposal in 1800 was to start taking Afrikan children away from their parents, to be held for disposal somewhere else. Meanwhile under his dream, aging Afrikan adults would continue living out their lives working away to profit white people. In 40 or 50 years no Afrikans would be left in the u.s. *"The old stock would die off in the ordinary course of nature... until its final disappearance."* Jefferson said god had "blessed" his plan.

The secret Jefferson Plan was never put into effect until now, because white amerikkka couldn't do without Black labor to support it. Now, they think their time has come.

YOU'RE NEVER TOO YOUNG IN AMERIKKKA TO BE A BLACK PRISONER

It all starts with the children and with white women. Black Genocide wouldn't work without white women, who are the hidden key to it. You know, we say genocide is a male military thing, men's deeds alone: In Germany the gestapo in uniforms, with submachine guns, ordering all the Jews out of their houses into trucks and trains. There's never any German women in the picture. But that's not how genocide started, only how it ended.

In Germany the campaign to wipe out the Jews began against the children. German women began organizing during the 1920s to stop their children from associating with Jewish children. Mothers warned their children to stay away from all Jews. Jews were characterized as not only "subhuman" animals, but very dangerous criminals and perverts who wanted to get pure white children into their hands. It was white women's mission, the Nazis said, to protect their families by keeping the "Jew" away.

Shoppers' boycotts of Jewish stores and demands that Jewish children be sent to separate schools were conducted by German women. The movement to push Jews out of every part of German life began with children in the home, and as it gathered strength it extended to the schools, to blocks and then neighborhoods, to rural towns and small cities, then to workplaces.

Only then did the government begin to strip the Jewish people of first legal rights and then of German citizenship. The Jewish reservations (death camps) were not the first but the last stage in a complex genocidal machinery.

Violent attacks and terrorism against Jews, at first isolated incidents, grew in number over the years. Nazis shouted that they were only protecting German women and children, that Jewish criminality and animal-like behavior forced good Germans to defend themselves.

The idea of violence against Jews began to be accepted as normal, just part of life. For years the police pretended to be trying to protect Jews (just like the u.s. police), although it could be seen that many more Jews and revolutionaries were being arrested than Nazis.

After 1933 the police and the Nazis merged, with beating and killings of Jews being done under police protection. It wasn't until nine years after that and 20 years after it all began, when the Jewish community had been already pushed out, dazed and ground down, in 1941, that death camps could begin.

While German revolutionary women died trying to stop the Nazis, most German women either supported genocide or said that it was men's affairs and had nothing to do with them. **This was the position adopted by the middle-class white feminist movement.**

Striving for equal rights with their men was the program of the women's movement, which argued that German feminists shouldn't be distracted from their own concerns by what it defined as male political issues (genocide, fascism). And armed struggle against imperialism was viewed by the women's movement with horror, as unfitting their view of the gentle, nonviolent nature of civilized white women (kind of like the delicate Southern belle and her mate, the slavemaster).

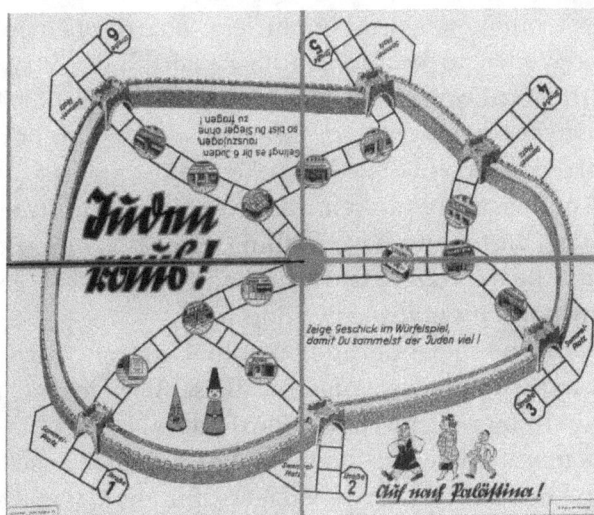

"Get the Jews Out!" children's board game. The child who wins has chased six Jews from their homes and businesses (shown by the circle in the center). Even though there are five exits only one has a road which leads to Palestine. The rhyming instructions read, "Be skillful when the dice you throw—and you'll collect Jews by the droves—If you succeed in throwing six Jews out—You're the winner without a doubt."

IT'S ALL IN THE FAMILY

Nazism was indeed a male movement, in which even Nazi
women held a very subordinate position. But it was dependent upon women. It was women who made genocide possible. Not only were women men's invaluable supporters,
loyally taking care of their Nazi husbands and raising Nazi
children, but they played the frontline role in the early stages
of genocide. Without women's help, active and passive, the
Nazis could never have justified genocide as necessary for
the defense of the white family and children.

And how are amerikkkan women different from those
German women?

On April 20, 1987, a small brick house at 171-27 Glad-
win Avenue, Fresh Meadows, Queens, was torched to stop
the City from moving in six homeless "boarder babies," who
were presumed to be Black. Rita Amato, the woman who
heads the local white citizens council, said happily: *"When I
saw what happened to the house I was relieved."* Amato has since
been arrested as one of the five who did the arson.

Another white woman who lives across the street told
reporters: "Listen, we have nothing against babies. But the
mothers, the dope addicts. My husband says, we will never be
safe anymore. It's nothing but dopists."

And the neighborhood white children have been
taught to imagine how dangerous these Black infants might
be. One sixth-grade girl at the local Catholic school thought
it was a moral dilemma: "It's good, but it's bad. Those babies
could grow up to be rowdy teenagers. But then, they need to
sleep somewhere–you know?"

That was a lot better than the 11-year old boy who asked
a reporter: "Are they still going to be here when they grow
up?" ...What if they were, asked the reporter to whom he had
posed the question. Richard shrugged: "Well, I mean this
is a peaceful neighborhood, not noisy. I mean, they're not

Rita Amato and James Raffa as they are taken to court on charges that they were part of a group who set fire to an unoccupied house that was to be used as a foster home for infants.

brats. Not really brats. But growing up without parents they wouldn't be the same, you know?"

Only 11 years old, and already he has been taught the twisted rationalizations for pushing Black people out.

This is a big theme with white women, how they and their families are endangered unless Black people are kept far away. Black people, even infants, are said to be the aggressors. White people when they torch buildings and shoot and conduct hate campaigns are said to only be defending themselves. Like the Germans did. Building the public mood that excuses and prepares people to commit genocide. **If even six Black infants without parents are too dangerous, what is safety?** What is the logical conclusion?

It's even more interesting how some prominent white women have come out making excuses for the terrorists. Queens Borough President Claire Shulman said that it was the government's fault for not reassuring the local homeowners that no adult Black people would be moved in: *"Otherwise, they imagine the worst. These are our people, our citizens. You can't ride roughshod with them, and they're afraid."*

Lynda Spielman, chairperson of Community Board 7, said that the firebombing was caused by "frustration" from the City's high-handed attitude. Violent whites are again pictured as the victims not the criminals.

KIDNAP & CONTROL

Most interesting of all was "feminist" newspaper columnist Beth Fallon in the *New York Post.* Her column stated that the real issue is tighter white control over Black people. This column was valuable precisely because it starts to take the wraps off:

> *The City is being overwhelmed by the sheer numbers of people who are unable or unwilling to care for themselves or their children, and who abandon the latter to the care of the state...*

> *City officials have said that family visits, if any, and visits of prospective foster parents for these infants would be at neutral sites away from the home.*

> *It is the unscheduled visits that evoke part of the neighborhood's fears, and it is these which should be met with immediate, effective control...*

> *The issue of control is really the deciding one...*

> *Staten Island, indeed, prefers to accept a prison site to sites for the homeless. More control is exercised at a prison, and the threat to the community is therefore perceived as less.*

This isn't hard to de-code: the government should reassure the white majority by "immediate, effective control" of any Black persons who enter white areas. Perhaps by police pass-books, like in South Africa? Facilities for Black people should become more like prisons, for "more control" is needed. Any uncontrolled Black people are a threat, and presumably white people are justified in defending themselves.

And this is a woman newspaper columnist.

It isn't one journalist who is just loosely mouthing off. There's a real convergence here. The *New York Times* has taken up the demand for more prison-like control over Black people. In an editorial about the "NIMBY syndrome" ("Not in My Back Yard"), the most influential newspaper in the u.s. has called for all new homeless shelters to include a built-in police station, so that homeless Black people would be under 24-hour police watch to reassure white people: *"What's to be done to ease Nimby apprehensions? One response is to introduce a round-the-clock police presence in each of the new facilities. Storefront offices could serve as police sub-stations…"*

The welfare system and the prison system are really only one system.

You should see now what the logical conclusion of this propaganda is, what it is pointing white people towards. Someday everyone will see it, but you should see it now. Time is a thing.

If the white majority wants to push Black children out, do the welfare agencies and their group homes represent a decent white alternative? No, for the same reason that Malcolm X used to say that integration is not the opposite of segregation, only a different version of the same thing.

In the wake of the firebombing, Mayor Koch rushed out to the Queens house to hold a public meeting. He told local whites, as press and TV surrounded him, that each white neighborhood must overcome its reluctance towards government facilities for Black poor and homeless:

"They all think they're being asked to do more than everybody else. We are trying to spread the burden."

Beth Fallon and Mayor Koch are saying that Black people are too dangerous to have children. That white people and their government have to be in control over Black children. That Black children have to be taken away. And this is how the Jefferson Plan begins.

BORDER BABIES

Those Black infants aren't "boarder babies," they're really border babies. Some of the hundreds of thousands of Black children being kidnapped by the government, and taken across the border into white amerikkka as prisoners. **Because in "America" you're never too young to be a Black prisoner.**

Government foster care, youth residences, welfare hotels, juvenile centers, riker's island, attica, isn't it all the same chain?

The government takes custody of Black children to kill them, to mess them up as much as possible so they will kill each other. Isn't that what happens?

That's what was going down around the border babies, before anguished hospital workers leaked the word out. The government had no plans to do anything for the 300 Black and Latino border babies in City hospitals. Without mothers or without mothers with homes, the homeless infants lay in metal cribs, lined up in rows.

Actually there was a plan. To secretly let them die. If a Nazi officer had tried to let 300 infants die he'd be called a war criminal. But when Mayor Koch does it all the whites curse him for being too "liberal."

Without close human contact, without care, babies suffer developmental damage and death. This is a medical fact. Yet the government was leaving these infants to die in isolation. That's a fact, too. Overworked nurses were trying to spend a few minutes with each, on the run. Dr. Margaret Heagarty, director of pediatrics at Harlem Hospital, protested to the press in May 1987:

"I have children whose parents are dead, and I have no one to teach them how to walk."

The government wasn't interested in these children learning how to walk, since they are Black. For Black children they have a special program: genocide.

In June 1987, to stop a lawsuit, the City signed a consent agreement in Federal court promising to get all border babies out of the hospital wards in six months or so. Mayor Koch and his bureaucrats plan to set up over 60 more government-run group homes to hold them (there were already over 50 at the time). Social worker slang calls these City group homes "parking lots," which tells us something.

The group that sued the City, the Association to Benefit Children, said publicly that the government agreed in negotiations to as little as possible, and had "kicked and screamed" over "every inch of it." We only want Black children to die, as cheaply and quietly as possible. And they say that because Black people are so messed up, white people must have more and more control over Black children, must take these children away.

You're Never Too Young In ameriKKKa To Be A Black Prisoner

An infant at Harlem Hospital.

Aren't there already many thousands of Black children in government custody in New York City alone? (Not even counting those in juvenile prisons.) All are suffering for it. A majority of the 18,000 foster care children are Black or Puerto Rican, prisoners of a system that the *NY Times* was forced to describe this year in the following terms:

> *And a tragedy of major proportions is occurring each day, according to interviews with participants throughout the system… physical abuse of children has become a daily occurrence.*

These foster care kids are shuffled without any say from place to place, lose what friendships and ties they have, have little opportunity for education, undergo beatings and sexual abuse. If one, just one, u.s. white man was held in Vietnam or Nicaragua under the conditions that thousands of these children are tortured with, congressmen would be lining up to threaten airstrikes.

You're never too young in amerikkka to be a Black prisoner. Face the fact that there are more Black children prisoners than Black adult prisoners in New York. And so the Jefferson Plan begins.

Today there are 9,000 children, the great majority of them Black, doing time in the welfare hotels. The schools admit that 50% are absent any given day. Young as they are, these kids are being brutalized, being conditioned to be the future drug addicts, the homeless, and prison inmates. The system understands this very well.

> *In the cavernous ballroom of the Princes George Hotel, four boys were shooting pool, talking as tough as any New York pool sharks. One wore just his shorts, and another's face was smeared with sweat. With the boys as old as 12, they might have seemed wise about the streets—except that two of them were sucking their thumbs.*

Tomorrow morning they'll be sucking a bottle or a jumbo to ease their pain or sticking the glass dick in their veins.

> *There are 8,980 children in the hotels. They are crammed four, six or seven to a room and eat one hot meal a day.*

Children are beautiful with possibilities to become anything. A carpenter or a freedom fighter, an artist or a scientist, anything. But these children are being conditioned to be nothing, to kill each other and themselves. To be in attica, to die of AIDS, or to be on drugs when they grow up. In fact, some children from the shelters, welfare hotels and other homeless children have been pushed into prostitution for survival. To serve white men.

ED & HIS JOHNS

Amerikkka is practicing its version of equal rights, since the children are half girls and half boys. The overwhelming majority of these child prostitutes are Black and Latino. The "Johns" who use them are largely middle-class and upper-class white men.

And the police say that except for token arrests there's nothing they can do about it (although last year they did arrest 229 homeless children from age 11 for prostitution). *"In a few years, we will be seeing lots of kids die from AIDS"* because of this prostitution, says child advocate Trudee Able-Peterson.

After unfavorable publicity on national TV about this child prostitution in 1985, Mayor Ed Koch ordered the police to set up a special undercover task force. He promised at a press conference to end the problem. That was in October 1985.

Ten months later the NYPD reported that their undercover task force to cover the Times Square-Port Authority bus
terminal area had managed to arrest 74 men for soliciting for
child prostitution, an average of only 7 arrests per month.

How many "Johns" were sent to prison in ten months?
Only two. Of the 53 cases that were decided by the time of the
report, 4 were dismissed and 43 men were allowed to plea-
bargain down to a lesser charge (mostly disorderly), paid a
small fine and walked. Only 6 men were convicted of soliciting for child prostitution. One man got probation and three
men were sentenced to the time awaiting trial, and walked.
Only two "Johns" who must have been the wrong class, were
sentenced to some prison time.

Buying a Black child for sex is being all but legalized,
a minor noncrime like running a red light. And yet, white
amerikkka says Blacks should turn their children over to us.

You know, there's a special "Black desk" at NYPD
Intelligence Division to spy on the Black community. Cops
are busy monitoring Black radio programs ("What are those
slaves up to?"). Busy following around the handful of Black
political activists. But so long as white men want Black and
Latino children, the government winks at their own laws. We
should name the procurer supplying Black children as prostitutes—amerikkka. These young victims have really been
kidnapped by white amerikkka.

WELFARE IS WARFARE

The entire point of the government welfare bureaucracy is
to stop the Black Nation from itself taking care of its children, to hinder and regulate and prohibit and confuse and
seize.

How long do you think it would take the Black community to end the open prostitution of Black children, were it not for the police protecting the white men? A week? You don't think all the police around mid-town Manhattan are there to protect the children, do you?

Everyone knows that once, not too long ago, there were few homeless Black children. Even though Black poverty was just as heavy then as now. The strong communal tradition among Afrikan people meant that women simply took in children that needed care. Whether blood relatives or neighbors, every Black child was kin.

There are many white women who make a living out of the disguised prison system for Black kids, as social workers and supervisors and therapists.

White women are, in fact, indispensable to the genocide of Black children, for it must be done with a thin veneer of official "caring." These are the so-called welfare institutions, which make such a show of helping the people that they mess over. **Ever notice the more we "help" them the worse off they are?**

It's the Hottest Game of the Year! Order Now!

One day, two small businessmen were trying to figure how to meet their payrolls; complaining about high taxes and other inequities in our system which seem to penalize the hard-working person and reward the able-bodied welfare recipients. It was so much fun, they created a game that spoofs the free hand-outs, welfare cheats and soft government jobs. The pitfalls for the "Public Assistance" player is not to land in jail but landing in "Working Person's Rut" where you get hit by big bills and IRS. The big payoff is the government "cake walk" where the only science-stricken.

It's absolutely outrageous and you'll get some belly-laughs when you discover some of the wild things some people do to avoid going to work. After the game and its inventors were seen on the Today Show, they were swamped with calls. Articles were written in the Daily News, Time magazine, People magazine and many more. It created so much excitement and controversy you probably won't be able to get it at your local toy store.

amerikkkan board game from the 1980s, part of the white right resurgence and attack on welfare that would culminate in Bill Clinton "ending welfare as we know it" in 1996.

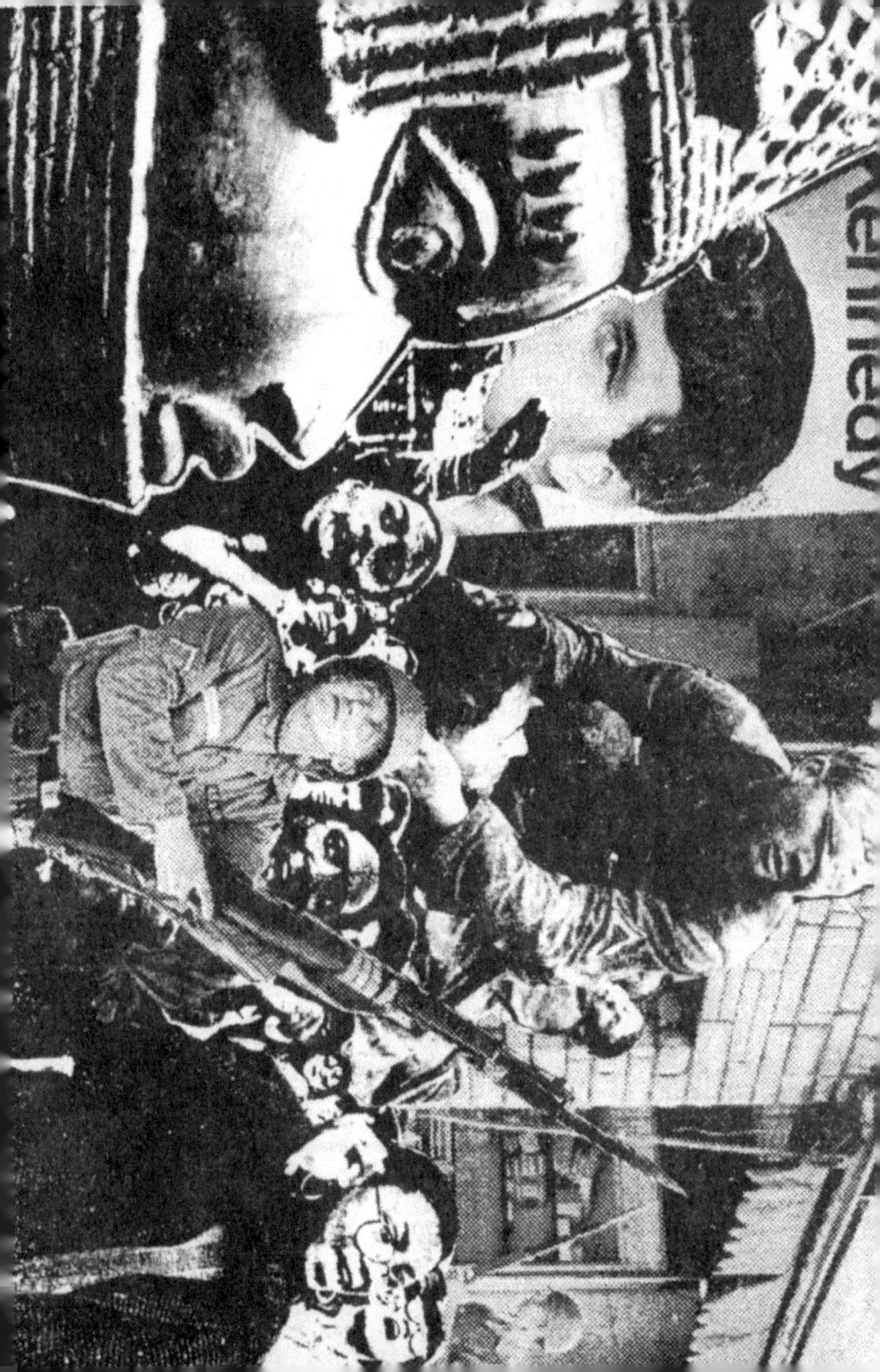

1968: YEAR OF DECISION

It's hard for people to see the whole strategy for Black genocide, because it doesn't come from the day before yesterday.
The ruling class decision to seek a Final Solution to their
"Black Problem" came from the 1960s. For it was in the Sixties
that amerikkka first lost its white-fisted grip on the world.

First, the patriarchy found itself in deep shit in Vietnam.
Something the latest fad of Vietnam war movies doesn't do
justice to. Hard to remember now that way back in 1965, as
the first battalions of marines waded ashore near Danang,
that the pentagon was promising that 50,000 u.s. troops
would finish off Charlie. They thought that the Vietnamese
would be a pushover, a small nation of small people, without
B-52s, IBM or John Wayne.

But the Vietnamese were a nation with a long history of
fighting invaders. While they didn't have John Wayne or the
national football league, they had something real like the
Truong sisters. Two amazons who led a war against the vast
Chinese empire a thousand years ago (the two are Vietnam's
national heroines). amerikkkans are creampuffs, in comparison. So five hundred thousand troops later the ruling class
got this sinking feeling that it was going to lose a war, and not
against a major white power but to an asian socialist army.

**What really did it to them was the danger of losing
amerikkka itself.**

Because amerikkka was exploding at home, and Black
people were at the heart of the storm riding it higher and
higher. In five, fast-frame years Civil Rights became Black
Power, and Black Power became Black Revolution. Nonviolent
student Sit-Ins faded into sniperfire and the burning buildings of ghetto uprisings. Hundreds protesting became thousands marching became millions "rioting."

Suddenly, the patriarchal ruling class saw a coming
Vietnam at home. City streets were shifting under the feet of

the world's strongest imperial patriarchy, who had believed that the Civil Rights sops of 1963 would buy them out of the shit. Black leaders selected and owned by the patriarchy were driven off the streets along with their white masters. It wasn't going to hold. There had to be an end, a permanent solution.

MOTOWN EXPLODES

Detroit, the new center of Black music, became a symbol. On July 23, 1967 at 3:30 am, a police raid on an afterhours club led to instant rumors that a Black woman had been beaten. A gathering crowd in the early morning started throwing bottles at the police paddy wagon. The growing crowd spread up and down 12th street. Breaking store windows, repossessing merchandise, and burning them out. The festival grew and grew as the people ruled the streets.

In six days forty-three people were killed, 2,000 wounded, and 7,000 arrested in Detroit. There were 1,442 fires recorded by the fire department. Even the Michigan National Guard was not enough. White order was not restored until President Lyndon Johnson sent in combat-seasoned u.s. army airborne troops, which took back the ghetto block by block.

Detroit's auto factories became simmering battlegrounds in 1968–69 for the new Black Revolutionary Union Movement. A majority of Black auto workers in the local Chrysler plants, at the Jefferson Ave. plant, at Dodge Eldon Ave. gear & axle plant, voted for this Black nationalist union and its program of socialism. It stood for aligning the Black Nation with Vietnam, Afrika, and the rest of the Third World against white amerikkka.

A Revolutionary Union Movement mass walkout at one plant proved that they could even shut down the production line. The ruling class couldn't believe that this strange nightmare was happening to them. Even high wages amerikkkan-style weren't enough to satisfy the mood for extreme change, for a new life. *"Liberation,"* one Sixties slogan went, *"is coming from a Black thing."*

This revolutionary trend of looking to politically leave amerikkka was at the heart of the storm. After the summer rebellions of 1967, government researchers interviewing Black youth in Newark, NJ found that 52.8% opposed backing the u.s. in any war, not just Vietnam.

BLACK NATION—WHITE PANIC

For the ruling class the decisive line was crossed when New Afrikan voices began formulating the demand for land. Not just acres and neighborhoods, but the raising up of the Black Nation. In 1968 Black revolutionary nationalists set the goal as the takeover of the five historic Black-majority states of the old Slave South: Louisiana, Mississippi, Alabama, Georgia and South Carolina. And then secession of their Republic of New Afrika from amerikkka. Remember, Vietnam was proving that the u.s. could be defeated by a smaller Third World nation. In the Sixties so many barriers had fallen, the unthinkable had happened so regularly, that anything felt possible.

The plan of carving a sovereign Black Nation out of amerikkka shocked white people and seemed crazy to them, but the ruling class knew that it had an explosive potential. In 1969 a poll by Newsweek magazine of Northern Black people under age 30 found that 68% approved of "Black

Power," 36% thought that Black political violence was necessary, and 27% wanted to live in a separate Black Nation. And already, the first generation of Black urban guerrillas was appearing.

A certain line, unseen and yet very real, had been crossed. Black labor had been the most important source of profit for amerikkka's ruling class ever since the original 13 colonies. But the ruling class decided during the 1960s that Black people were just too dangerous to have around (a common feeling whites often have).

Clashes following police murder of 15-year old
New Afrikan James Powell, Harlem 1964.

MOYNIHAN-ISM:
THE ATTACK ON BLACK WOMEN

The crux of the matter is that to destroy the Black Nation you have to destroy Black women. And you have to convince white women that it's ok. Women are the key in both instances.

For all the white fright about Black men, the cool heads in the ruling dickdom know that black men aren't their only or even biggest problem. Everyone knows that Black women are the heart and backbone of the Black Nation and its communities. They are the protectors of its children, its continuity and of its traditions of resistance.

Afrikan and New Afrikan men, like all men the world over, share the his-story and distortions of having ruled over or desiring to rule over women and children, of feeling right about themselves by physically subduing half the human race and then defeating each other, of getting over on each other, having more than the next guy. These distortions are hard to overcome. The exact things that men feel make them strong, in reality make them weak in the face of genocide.

Singling out Black women as the No. 1 target started with Daniel Patrick Moynihan in the mid-1960s. Since Moynihanism has reared its pricky head again, this has special importance to the patriarchal ruling class.

Our story begins with the release of the Moynihan Report in June 1965, before the decision for Black Genocide was reached. The Report placed the main trouble of the Black community on women-headed families, which the Report said were un-amerikkkan and sick ("a tangle of pathology").

Moynihan was one of the four white men who had planned out the details of President Johnson's War on Poverty. His Report, which became so infamous, was not originally meant to be seen by the public. It was an internal

policy paper, given to less than eighty men in the top levels
of the Administration.

His action proposals were staggering: **the White House
should review every government program, including federal hiring and the military, to make certain that in every
way Black men get preference over Black women.** Moynihan
wanted a massive Federal men's jobs program. One study of
his proposals summed it up:

> *In the area of concrete programs, Moynihan felt that jobs
> had primacy and that the government should not rest
> until every able-bodied Negro man was working even if
> this meant that some women's jobs had to be redesigned to
> enable men to fulfill them.*

This was a big-stakes game. Daniel Patrick Moynihan, who
was then Assistant Secretary of Labor, thought that the government was underestimating the crisis.

He worried that President Johnson and his closest advi-
sors had been lulled into thinking that the "Negro revolution" was over, that the Democrats had won Black people's
loyalty and trust for the next 100 years. Moynihan was predicting to the contrary, in Fall 1964, that the Civil Rights Act
wasn't going to satisfy the Black community, and that even
bigger uprisings ("riots") were coming.

His report begins by reminding his fellow officials how
much is at stake, that the power balance of the world was
being fought out:

> *The Negro American revolution is rightly regarded as the
> most important domestic event of the postwar period in
> the United States...*
>
> *It was not a matter of chance that the Negro movement
> caught fire in America at just that moment when the
> nations of Africa were gaining their freedom. Nor is it*

merely incidental that the world should have fastened its attention on events in the United States at a time when the possibility that the nations of the world will divide along color lines seems suddenly not only possible, but even imminent.

(Such racist views have made progress within the Negro-American community itself... The Black Muslim doctrines, based on total alienation from the white world, exert a powerful attraction. On the far left, the attraction of Chinese communism can no longer be ignored.)

MORE SEXISM THE U.S. PLAN

To neutralize the "attraction" of revolutionary alternatives, Moynihan wanted the Black community to be made more sexist, more "American." He identified the strength of Black women as the main enemy. Even more, Moynihan believed that by the government giving Black men power over Black women, by giving Black men jobs that were held by Black women whether in the P.O. or in the schools and by making

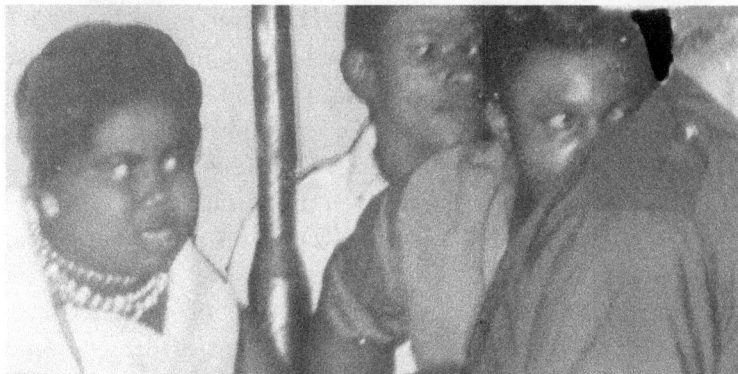

Black men heads of families, that the government could pacify the ghetto in a way acceptable to white voters. No white men's jobs would be threatened, for example.

The government, Moynihan said, could now blame Black women for the oppression of all Black people. Black women could be propagandized against as the Black man's own worst enemy. And Black progress, Moynihan said, can only come through sexism:

> *In essence, the Negro community has been forced into a matriarchal structure which, because it is so out of line with the rest of the American society, seriously retards the progress of the group as a whole, and imposes a crushing burden on the Negro male...* ***Ours is a society which presumes male leadership in private and public affairs. The arrangements of society facilitate such leadership and reward it. A subculture, such as that of the Negro American, in which this is not the pattern, is placed at a distinct disadvantage.***

This was pretty upfront. Black people weren't sexist enough to fit into amerikkka.

Moynihan made the crucial point that Black women have been unfit mothers, damaging their children. As he wrote "Negro children without fathers flounder and fail."

He introduced some phony statistics to prove that Black children raised by women without a husband in the house have a low IQ. Moynihan said that these Black children were on average of "dull-normal" IQ, just above retarded. Black women were the enemy of Black children, too, he was suggesting. This tactic was to be even more important later.

In the Report, Moynihan was careful about how he made the point that Black mothers mess over male children. Cautiously, he made his point by using prominent Black bourgeois men. Whitney Young, president of the National Urban League, was quoted saying: "In the matriarchal Negro society, mothers made sure that if one of their children had a chance at education the daughter was the one to pursue it." Social scientist Thomas Pettigrew was quoted:

> *Many Negro mothers often act to perpetuate the mother-centered pattern by taking a greater interest in their daughters than their sons.*

Moynihan and his staff at the Office of Policy Planning & Research finished the Report in March 1965. Only one hundred copies were made. On May 4, 1965 his superior, Labor Secretary Willard Wirtz, gave the President a memorandum by Moynihan summing up the Report. That summer it was made evident by burning buildings that Moynihan was right about their "Black problem" not being solved. The White House decided to support his action proposals.

In June the Report was released to the public, and was a major news story. Then it became a major controversy. The White House convened a national conference of officials, social scientists, religious and Civil Rights leaders to rally the Black community behind Moynihan's "pro-family" program. This was to be the final chapter in President Johnson's War on Poverty.

Daniel Patrick Moynihan

MOYNIHAN-ISM STEPS IN IT

That 1965 White House Conference collapsed into a political disaster area after the first day. Under angry Black community pressure, the Civil Rights leaders got wishy-washy about committing themselves to follow Moynihan. Some, like the Urban League's Whitney Young, who had been happy about the Moynihan program at first, began backing out as public criticism rose higher and higher.

Within a few months the Moynihan Report was abandoned by the White House, too burnt-up to use. Dissenters within the Black community had exposed it as nothing but a sneaky attempt to blame the oppressed for their oppression, to turn attention away from institutionalized racism. Many Black women were furious that their families were called "pathological." Moynihan became discredited as a racist in sheep's clothing.

When the uprisings kept coming in 1965, in 1966 and 1967, kept growing, when even men with good-paying jobs on the auto assembly lines joined Black nationalist rifle clubs and took part in uprisings, then the imperialists knew that it was too, too late for the speeches about Abraham Lincoln.

New Afrikan youth taunt police, Harlem uprising 1964.

RULING CLASS PULLS ITS SWITCH

And as the intractable nature of their "Black problem" became clearer, the ruling class itself vetoed all of Moynihan's
proposals. Moynihan and the Lyndon Johnson White House
had thought they could turn the clock back. They thought
that they could restore peace by remaking the Black community into a poorer, 2nd class version of traditional 1940s or
1950s white culture—*father working and ruling the roost, mother
kept at home waiting on men and raising lots of children for the ruling class, children kept in line by authoritarian father.*

The Moynihan program got trashed mostly because
the patriarchal ruling class decided that it could no longer
live with the threat of Black revolution. It wasn't going to hire
any millions of young Black men. No way, forget that. It was
going to start drawing up a whole new set of plans, do that
Black Genocide. Can't trust them, gotta dust them.

*Moynihan's mistake was that he saw this as a civilian prob-
lem, a social problem. The ruling class more correctly saw their
"Black problem" as a political-military problem, needing military
solutions.*

Daniel Patrick Moynihan thought that with a few middle-class jobs and titles, a little Civil Rights sprinkled on top,
having Black men rule over "their" women, that the Black
community would be brought back into place as one of
amerikkka's profitably subject peoples. But Moynihan, who
saw President Johnson's underestimations, underestimated
the crisis himself.

This was a time when, despite historic white reforms,
millions of Black people wanted a separate nation of their
own. The Nation of Islam, which was the movement of a
separate Black society headed by Elijah Muhammad and
Malcolm X, had gained an estimated five million adherents.
Black revolutionaries were hijacking airliners and going into
exile in Cuba. College students and factory workers alike

were reading revolutionary theorists from the Third World, Franz Fanon and Mao and Amilcar Cabral. Millions of Black high school students were taking part in school walkouts and boycotts.

This ruling class could only deal with this crisis in a political-military way, by deciding on the final solution of Black Genocide. Moynihan caught on quickly. In the Nixon years he helped lead the government campaign to forcibly empty the ghetto–he coined the infamous phrase of "benign neglect," to justify the government's urban removal and unemployment strategy.

Maybe Daniel Moynihan got a black eye out of the controversy, but the ruling class found him useful and put their arm around him. After having been a top official for the liberal Kennedy and Johnson administrations, Moynihan was kept around as a key urban policy advisor by the conservative Nixon administration. From there he went on to be a u.s. senator. Not bad for someone who's one big idea was a flop. Amerikkka's ruling class needed his talent for dumping on Black women but making it sound like intellectual theorizing about poverty.

Another reason Moynihan-ism never died is that it played on the chords of sexism within the Black community. Don't forget that the White House only agreed to risk that public conference because Moynihan had gotten private agreement from many Black leaders. His sexist theories about the harmful Black "matriarchy" were borrowed A to Z from the writings of Black sociologist E. Franklin Frazier of Howard University. Even that zingy line that most angered Black women–of their families being only "a tangle of pathology"–was only Moynihan quoting E. Franklin Frazier.

Poor Moynihan felt betrayed, double-crossed by all his Black male colleagues who encouraged him to go for it, then after the shit hit the fan pretended that they had nothing to do with his report.

Following the 1967 Detroit uprising, President Johnson appointed a blue-ribbon panel of establishment social scientists, politicians, generals, policemen, corporate leaders and Civil Rights flunkies, to recommend what to do.

That was the National Advisory Commission on Civil Disorders, better known as the Kerner Commission after its chairman, Otto Kerner (he was former Illinois governor and part of the Chicago Democratic Party machine). Racism was strongly denounced in the Commission's report, which called for the immediate integration of housing and employment.

But what they called "housing integration" was only the public front for the counter-insurgency assault that the Kerner Commission consultants named Spatial Deconcentration. There is an old saying that "the best place to hide something is in plain sight." The Kerner Commission provided a smooth public cover for an unprecedented coming together of the u.s. leadership. Corporate heads and police chiefs, generals and bankers, urban strategists and cabinet officials, all sat down together in day after day strategy sessions on the inner cities.

The Commission had put its finger on a major military consideration: the massive weight of heavily-populated Black

It took the National Guard and u.s. Army five days to suppress the Detroit uprising: the official figures were 43 dead, 1,189 injured, over 7,200 arrests, and more than 2,000 buildings destroyed.

ghettoes, all within easy striking distance of white down-
towns. White House, Wall St. & Mercantile Exchange, City
Hall & Police HQ, banks and corporate skyscrapers, were all
next door targets for urban guerrilla warfare. And the sheer
size of Black communities made uprisings hard to prevent
or control.

So the secret proposal of the Kerner Commission was
to break up the giant ghettoes, to physically bulldoze and
burn the Black community completely out of existence. No
community, no uprisings, was their simple equation. Under
the long-range Spatial Deconcentration plan, the Black population is to be widely dispersed, scattered into small pockets
around the county (reservations, in other words) where they
would be more easily policed.

Naturally, the Kerner Commission presented this plan
as "housing integration," a civil rights measure to supposedly help Black people. Spatial Deconcentration had two
parts: The first was to resettle Black families out in new suburban or rural housing projects. Unlike in the inner cities,
in the suburbs pockets of Black people would be isolated
and surrounded by larger numbers of whites. Urban theorist
Anthony Downs, who actually wrote chapters 16 and 17 of
the Kerner Report, warned the government to develop "a
workable mechanism ensuring that whites will remain in the
majority."

The main hammer-blow of Spatial Deconcentration is
the physical elimination of major Black urban communities,
to force Black families to break up and disperse. Anthony
Downs later wrote that the plan is "a long-range strategy of
emptying-out the most deteriorated areas... to accelerate
their abandonment."

This has proved easy to do: deliberate non-enforcement
of building codes, police-controlled drug epidemics, urban
renewal, and covert firebombing campaigns. Each year there
is less and less housing for Black children, each year more

of the Black community breaks apart under the gradually tightening encirclement of Black Genocide.

All part of the military counter-insurgency move of "drying up the sea." From the analogy where the revolutionary guerrillas are the "fish" and the oppressed communities they come from are the "sea" that shelters and nourishes them. In both Vietnam and El Salvador, u.s. forces used constant air bombardment to force the people to break up and migrate out of rebellious areas.

The idea is to make the community unliveable, by physical destruction of housing, by making it a violent "free fire zone" for government-sponsored gangs and police, by deliberately spreading epidemics of crack and AIDS, all to force masses of desperate people to "voluntarily" abandon their community and disperse.

Secretly, the ruling class has been firebombing the Black community, all without a single Pentagon document or congressional declaration of war. There has been a national wave of inner city fires since the 1960s. A 1979 headline says it all: "ARSON AT AN EPIDEMIC RATE, WITH 300% RISE IN 3 YEARS." All it takes is for the ruling class insurance companies to quietly put out their willingness to insure delapidated ghetto slums for big sums, while the police quietly make it known that landlord arson will be permitted.

That 1979 story says of 1,000 people killed each year in arsons, *"most of the victims are poor Blacks and Hispanic-Americans."* Secretly murdered by amerikkka.

As an example, the story tells about a Jersey City, NJ tenement, 358 York Road, where arson on January 22, 1979, killed five children and two adults. That was the 60th "suspicious fire" in two years in slum buildings owned by one slumlord, Kibby Kevelson. All insured. After the fires and insurance money, Kevelson sells his buildings to the government for urban renewal projects. No jail time for these slumlords, of course.

These emptied-out inner city communities are being gradually white-washed, or warehoused for years, and then gentrified for middle-class "integrated" housing and corporate development. New "Yuppie Harlem" is only the most obvious example.

One goal of the Spatial Deconcentration is to gradually resettle a solid white majority to protect the central cities for imperialism. This only works if the Black population declines. Middle-class white women, feminists and lesbians most specifically included, are being recruited to be "urban pioneers" for the patriarchal ruling class. Isn't that a great phrase, *"urban pioneers"*? The original white pioneers, we recall, invaded and stole Indian land, and did that genocide, too. **Black Genocide has become white women's equal opportunity.**

NEO-COLONIALISM:
CHANGE THE CLASS STRUCTURE

INTEGRATION was also the code-name given to the social restructuring of the Black Nation, which has increasingly cleaved the Black society into a 25% middle-class, 25% working-class and a 50% under-class. In the 20 year process the Black working class, once the huge majority, is being wiped out. It was seen by the ruling class as the main danger.

Isn't it hard to imagine that in 1968, Black workers made up 50% of all the u.s. automobile industry workforce, that Black workers had formed nationalist caucuses and joined their own revolutionary nationalist unions and called Black strikes? Northern urban factories that had a 40–80% Black labor force in the 1960s have been shut down, replaced by new factories abroad or in the rural South and Midwest.

Black youth who a generation ago would have become blue-collar workers are now forced down into the growing underclass. These are people who no longer have a place or role in the economy; they are permanently without real employment, in the hustling and welfare world. The world of death at an early age that is almost half the Black population today.

> *"Before the rebellion, a Black man in Detroit had a certain stability, a false sense of security," said the Rev. Albert B. Cleage Jr., founder of Shrines of the Black Madonna. "He now has no security whatsoever. The whole atmosphere in the Black community has become one of escapism. People use drugs and every kind of hustle and drugs to get by. The dope industry has taken over the excess people from the auto industry."*

The Black community's share of total u.s. income hasn't changed essentially since 1960, but it has been divided up very differently. The u.s. government temporarily forced corporations and local government to hire Black professionals as they were un-hiring Black workers. *"Between 1960 and 1970 the percentage of middle-class Blacks suddenly doubled, growing from about 1 in 8 to 1 out of every 4 Black workers,"* writes sociologist Bart Landry.

Integration has produced a new Black middle class that is being encouraged to transfer its loyalties out of the Black community. To live a white consumer lifestyle and reside in "integrated" middle-class housing. For awhile, anyway. Educated Black people are encouraged to distance themselves from the Black grassroots as much as possible, while the Black underclass is being encouraged to die as much as possible. This manipulation of the Black class structure is planned to socially fragment the Black community as a community, as it is simultaneously under physical assault by the strategy of Spatial Deconcentration. A political-military campaign is being masked as integration.

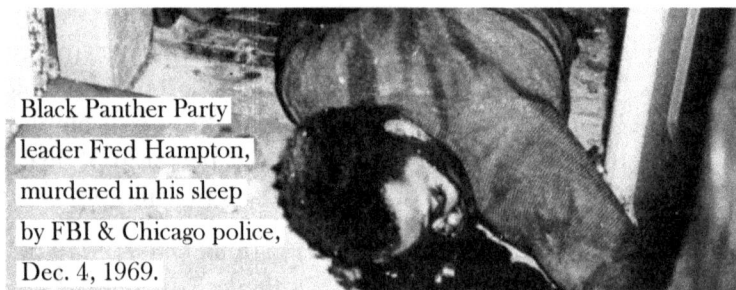

Black Panther Party leader Fred Hampton, murdered in his sleep by FBI & Chicago police, Dec. 4, 1969.

PHOENIX PROGRAM FOR GHETTO

In Vietnam the CIA ran a special war within the war: a covert program to paralyze the Vietnamese ability to resist invasion by assassinating peasant community leaders in each locality, village by village. Former CIA Director William Colby testified before Congress that his CIA "Phoenix Program" (which he had personally run in Saigon) had assassinated around 20,000 Vietnamese thought to be grassroots leaders and organizers; using informers, secret surveillance files, and specially trained u.s. assassination teams. This was denied officially at the time, and only admitted after the war had been lost.

Since the 1960s the CIA & FBI have been running an unadmitted "Phoenix Program" to neutralize Black resistance. Leaders thought too dangerous have been systematically killed or imprisoned. Black militant organizations have been eliminated. The Black Panther Party was cut down by coordinated police raids in 11 states. Over 1,000 BPP members were arrested throughout 1968–69. Many Black nationalist groups of the day were repressed. Thousands went to prison.

Front-page assassinations, such as Malcolm X and MLK Jr., were skillfully arranged to be done by cats-paws. So James Earl Ray, the Southern cracker who was let out of prison to shoot Martin Luther King, Jr., was said by the FBI to be a deranged "lone assassin." Although he was captured in London, England with three false passports and $15,000 in cash. How did he obtain that alone in prison, some skeptics asked?

The "Phoenix Program" operates on the principle that masses of people in motion can be handled by removing their leadership. The CIA always believed that if it had started this early enough it might have won in Cuba and Southeast Asia, and it isn't taking the same chance in the even more crucial war in amerikkka. Neutralizing revolutionary activists is not the main blow in genocide. But it is designed to neutralize people's natural ability to defend themselves against that main blow. Like destroying the body's immune defense system against infection.

GOOD GUYS vs. BAD GUYS

There is a white fight going on over the tactics of genocide. Black genocide is the biggest event in amerikkka, far too big to be neatly contained inside the Black community as white people want it to be. It spills over into everyone's lives in multiple ways. And white people, whose differing lives and economic interests are touched, inevitably are fighting over how to commit genocide. Who will pay the damage bills, who will profit most?

Mind you, there isn't any noticeable fight over the strategy of Black Genocide itself. It's only a white family squabble over the tactics of the matter. Sometimes this is a liberal vs. conservative fight, like uncle teddy vs. grandad ronnie. Or sometimes this is a ruling class vs. its white servants dispute, like Mayor Crazy Ed trying to get white racist homeowners in Queens to go along with kidnapping Black babies.

Only, the liberals want to do it gracefully, slick, with lots of p.r. and a minimum of damage to amerikkka. While the conservatives want to do it directly, to openly starve and imprison the Black Nation and let the chips fall where they may. But they both want "it", a final end to amerikkka's "Black problem."

That white family fight is why there hasn't been more dispersal of Black families out into the suburbs, as the Kerner Commission's Spatial Deconcentration plan called for. The ruling class had to retreat on some parts when its plan ran aground on white resistance.

Emptying-out the ghetto was first supposed to be tested in Chicago. Mayor Richard J. Daley, boss of the then most powerful political machine in the u.s., was impatient to secure Chicago as a white city. Daley announced that the city's giant housing projects, which in Chicago were built in rows of high-rises surrounding the downtown business district on three sides (the lake is the 4th side), would be gradually abandoned.

Black welfare families would be paid bonuses to relocate in new, smaller projects, which would be scattered ("integrated") in rural unincorporated areas well outside the city, like little Indian reservations.

Instant hysteria from middle-class suburbanites created such white-hot political reaction that the government had to back off in Illinois. White people were saying, "Move 100,000 Black welfare recipients out to our county? Hell no!" And the White House had changed hands; the Republicans refused to come up with the hundreds of millions of dollars Mayor Daley needed to pull the plan off. He died in office without seeing his most arrogant move get off the ground. The right wing didn't want to build more housing projects, it wanted to build prisons and expand the army.

The ruling class compromise was to go ahead and destroy the ghetto anyway, even without any temporary escape valves, letting displaced Black refugees spill over onto streets and downtown sidewalks. In NYC Mayor Crazy Ed keeps saying he doesn't want to build more housing in the ghetto, he wants to "share the burden" of homeless Black people with all the neighborhoods. Further away the better.

In an amusing flip-flop, the political representatives of the white homeowners, such as Queens Borough President Claire Shulman, want the government to keep Black people away; even if it means building some temporary housing for them in the Black community.

And now Manhattan real estate interests led by developer Donald Trump and the media, are echoing the same thing. Somehow, anyhow, they demand, the government must keep the unsightly, might-be dangerous, Black refugees and casualties created by war in amerikkka at a distance. Stop them from taking over the streets outside luxury hi-rises and corporate headquarters. Prison barges and homeless barges anchored to wharves are the latest proposals.

Labels like liberal and conservative have a certain tactical meaning, but can't hide the truth that white society has become united around Black Genocide. *Whites believe that it is no longer possible—or necessary—to tolerate the Black Nation and its people.*

FIRST LAW OF GENOCIDE: CRIMINALIZATION

Those who commit genocide must first become hardened to it, must be armored with a frenzy of rationalizations in which they are only victims righteously defending themselves. While the actual victims of genocide must be said to be the aggressors, like those "savage redskins" whose continent we accidently took while we were defending ourselves. This is the first law of genocide. Things must be turned upside down.

Often, it is said that the victims of genocide aren't really human like you and i, but are "subhuman" and "animalistic." So you really shouldn't worry about what happens to them. Which is why Adolf Hitler lectured the German people that "the Jews are indeed a race, but not a human race." Which is why Israeli Prime Minister Begin reassured his countrywomen that the Palestinian women being killed are "only beasts that walk on two legs."

u.s. Sen. Alfonse D'Amato of NY, in privately vetoing proposed funding for a housing project, was quoted by another government official as remarking: *We didn't do too well with the animal vote, did we? Isn't it the animals who live in these projects? They're not our people.*

Oppressors want the victims of genocide to be seen as the aggressors, as the dangerous "animals" threatening everyone. The Nazis spent twenty years convincing Germans

that Jews were the aggressors. Even rank-and-file Nazi women had to be argued into not wavering about genocide.

> *"Often, much too often, one hears it still, 'I find the fight against the Jews too severe. It does not seem right that the good Jews must suffer on account of their race',"* wrote Paula Silber, chief of the Nazi Coordinating Committee for Women's Affairs in a 1933 newsletter to her follow- ers. She went on, criticizing Nazi women for their "senti- mental gush to say that the other person is also a human being and feels and senses like ourselves."

That wasn't true, Silber harangued her women:

> *"The Jew with his quite different nature, his essential being unlike ours, is a subtle poison, since he always destroys what is necessary to our life. The Jew has always felt bound to conquer the best places in the sun, ruthlessly destroying what was in his way. If we are to be healed as a people... then we must free ourselves ruthlessly from that parasite just as the body must get rid of poison if it is to be healed."**

What you should know is that Black people are the Jews of amerikkka. Think about that, even if you don't like the comparison.

---

* This passage is quoted from: Claudia Koontz, *Mothers in the Fatherland* (NY: St. Martin's Press, 1987).

A CRIMINAL CLASS

It is a crime now to be a Black man in amerikkka. Like the Indian before him, the Black man, particularly the young Black man, is said by white people to be a "savage," an "animal," irrationally violent and always dangerous. Young Black men ages 16 to 19 years old account for 51% of all those arrested by police for violent crimes.

Anytime that a Black man is imprisoned or killed, the automatic assumption is that "he only got what he deserved." Black men are considered a criminal class, who must be pushed out to keep white people safe. And anything that is done to them, anything at all, is ok. Everyone is told to fear them, they are the threat.

It isn't just teenage muggers in a subway car. Black men have been criminalized as a whole. Samuel Johnson, who recently resigned as Assistant Attorney General of Vermont, says that white folks in the capital would *"lean over and lock their car doors when they saw me coming."*

People magazine reports:

> At colleges in or near a Black neighborhood, Black students – particularly men – may spend their entire college careers under suspicion from campus security. Sid Smith, a Black at Yale, says he is regularly stopped and asked to show an ID. "I'm used to it," he says...

Someday Black men will need a pass to be outside the reservation.

This is the thickening atmosphere in which six Black border babies are considered so threatening that their house must be firebombed by white community leaders and the police (who conveniently pulled their patrols out for two hours so it could be done).

Black men have been so successfully criminalized that it is now acceptable for some stores in Manhattan to refuse to serve them. The usual device is to keep the front door locked, with a buzzer that the customer pushes to be let in. But if a Black man is at the door, the store personnel flash a sign saying "by appointment only" and smile, refusing to open the door.

A clothing store owner was quoted in the press as saying: "I'm afraid race is the first thing in my mind. A young, dark-skinned boy is not likely to get in here." More prosperous stores, like in Soho, hire a Black rent-a-cop and tell him to keep everyone like himself out. No joke. Or rather, it's a sick joke, but it's true.

Willie Horton and Linda Taylor, archetypical Black criminals of the 80s onslaught

WHITE WOMEN ARE BEING MOLDED

Now, the thing these Manhattan stores have in common is that they're owned or managed by white women. While segregation of public places is supposed to be illegal, when it's posed as white women having to protect themselves from dark-skinned "animals" then it's all right. White women are used as the symbols of victimization, just like the Deep South used to say that they needed lynchings to protect white women. It isn't that these few stores are important in themselves; they are one more foot in the door, one more tool in getting us used to legal restrictions on the movements of Black people. A new day is coming.

White women, like Nazi women in the first stages of genocide against the Jews, are on the front lines. Only it's disguised as women's equal rights. The controversy earlier this year at Wellesley College outside Boston is an example of what's going on. Henrietta Holsman, a 1970 alumna of the exclusive women's college, had to resign from the board of trustees. Black women had begun protesting over a lecture by her on business management.

Ms. Holsman is the owner of Stockton Wire Products, a manufacturing firm in Los Angeles. She warned her white sisters it was hard finding good workers because Latinos are "lazy" and Black men would rather go "back to the street to earn more money" pushing drugs.

When you put your white toes in your big white mouth that way, instead of saying the same thing in an indirect way or in sociolo-gese, then the rules say you gotta resign (whether you're with the Los Angeles Dodgers or are a women's college trustee).

This wasn't merely one woman's racist slip, though, because white faculty and administrators rushed in to defend and praise trustee Holsman. She was only doing not too well what she was supposed to do, it looks like.

Professor Marshal Goldman of the economics department told reporters that when Holsman said Black men were drug pushers she was only "describing her real life experiences on the factory floor." He praised Ms. Holsman as a role model for young white women: "She is just the kind of person Wellesley is usually proud of. She is young, imaginative, a successful entrepreneur, and she was trying to share her experiences with other women."

We got the message, all right. Black men are the criminal class. Don't worry if there are no jobs for Black men, because they'd rather be criminals anyway. And don't pay Latinos too much because they're "lazy." This educational message brought to us courtesy of the faculty and administration of Ivy League Wellesley College for women.

And how are amerikkkan women different from those German women?

White women are being molded by the ruling class, just as German women were, to put their shoulders to the wheel of genocide, to help criminalize Black people. Since there are some women who will question, who will hesitate and even rebel, it has become the job of what is cynically called "the women's movement" to keep our minds in line. i don't want to hide the fact that i consider this an act by bought women against womankind.

Policewoman: I understand the police wives' reactions to men and women on patrol. I'm a jealous wife too. But the bond between partners is unique. It's close, nonsexual and nonromantic. People think the only kind of closeness is love. But my partner and I are pulling together in life-and-death situations." —Ms., October, 1975

WOMEN'S FAULT!

Amerikkka has not forgotten the Black woman in all this. Not at all. They have the place of honor in the criminalization of Black men.

You see, they say it's all Black women's fault. And the kidnapping of Black children, it's all their fault too. Remember Beth Fallon's column in the *NY Post*? "...people who are unable or unwilling to care for themselves or their children, and who abandon the latter to the care of the state." That's Black and Latina women she is talking about, although Fallon is a media pro and knows you can't use names. Her white readers fill in the names anyhow.

'Course, then they say that the reason there's a Black male criminal class is that Black women are so strong and dominating that their sons grow up mentally maladjusted. Really, that's what the ruling class keeps putting out, hoping that not only white folk but also Black people will believe it. Last year the *NY Times* ran an editorial on this:

> *Larry Davis allegedly shot six police officers during a gun battle last month. Shavod Jones shot a police officer in Central Park last summer and left him paralyzed. James Ramseur, now serving time for rape, was one of Bernard Goetz's victims in the subway shooting two years ago.*

> *All three, and millions of others less notorious, are among the legion of young Black men who terrify urban neighborhoods... The need to do something about such young men is a concern now because so little was done for them when they were children. Indeed, their behavior vividly recalls Daniel Patrick Moynihan's warning in 1965:*

> *"A community that allows a large number of young men to grow up in broken families, dominated by women, never acquiring any stable relationship to male authority...*

*That community asks for and gets chaos. Crime, violence,
unrest, disorder… is not only to be expected; it is very
near inevitable. And it is richly deserved."*

The patriarchal ruling class wants us to believe that the
criminalization of Black men had nothing to do with them.
Oh, no. They want everyone, including many Black people, to believe that it grew out of psychological problems
between Black women and Black men. That having strong
mothers makes criminals out of their sons. It's all women's
fault, as usual! Notice that they're talking openly about "millions… the legion of young Black men" who are criminals as
a class now.

u.s. Sen. Moynihan and the government insist that a
household without a man is "broken," like my old television
set. As if women leading families isn't as natural as mother
nature. Hey, even Jesus' father didn't stick around, you know.
i forgot, Jesus turned out to be a criminal, too—but it was
Mary's fault!

When the ruling class says that young Black men must
have some male authority, that's their way of saying more
white male authority, and they don't mean that they're taking Larry Davis home with them to suburban Westchester.
Amerikkka is going to "help" Black youth by putting them
into white male-run institutions—the military and the prisons. The biggest housing boom in amerikkka right now is ex-
panding the prison system to hold more and more Black men.

That *NY Times* editorial ends by saying that Black youth
need something like the Vietnam War-era military draft:

*It provided what many young Black men never experi-
ence: exhaustive physical training, stern discipline, male
authority figures, a sense of camaraderie and group
purpose, rewards for jobs well done.*

Is that a recruiting pitch for a gang?

PRISON: THE BLACK MAN'S HOUSING PROJECT

By zero coincidence, that same day the newspaper had a
story on the overcrowding crisis in the NY state prison system, whose population is hitting 40,000 for the first time in
history. State officials say that there is no limit in sight–other
than finances–to how many Black men will be imprisoned:
"You can't build your way out of this. That's the conclusion,"
said a state prison official. "The more you build, the more
they fill up." **Think about that statement.**

One move the story says the state is considering are
juvenile forced-labor camps, as a cheaper alternative to sending Black and Latino teens to the regular prisons. These "si-
berias" would be located in remote rural areas upstate: "The
emphasis in the state camps would be on a curriculum of
out-door labor and military-like discipline."

New York state, having already expanded its prison system by 10,000 inmates in only 4 years, has just passed an
emergency prison construction bill. In the next three years
they will build two 500-bed maximum security prisons, three
700-bed medium security prisons, and will convert a juvenile
facility into a 2,000-bed prison. New York City's own prison

U.S. STATE AND FEDERAL PRISON POPULATION, 1925-2012

system has grown by one-third to over 16,000 since 1983, is experiencing prison uprisings and court orders.

Mayor Koch is having two new 700-bed City prisons built far, far upstate near the Canadian border. When they built the Indian reservations they also placed them in remote areas to isolate the inmates.

Amerikkka has stopped building public housing, and has shifted the funds into building prisons for Black men. This is a stone fact. Prisons are to be the Black man's new public housing projects, his special place in the rapidly growing Black reservation system. Does that sound so extreme that it's impossible? Look at how in just a few years they've made young Black men from a working class into a criminal class. And think of what this means for the future. Think about what's happening to Black children.

"We have lost our children," said Rev. Floyd Rose of the Toledo NAACP. "When they get to high school age they are not in school and they are not in jobs, they are on the streets. By the year 2000 it is estimated that 70% of all Black men will be in jail, dead or on drugs, or in the throes of alcoholism."

The most profound effect of the criminalization of Black men is not external, however, but is internal. Is to sabotage people's minds. By convincing youth that they are criminals the ruling class re-injects the old colonial mentality only in a "rebellious" form.

Coming of age, they discover that the system has no place in it for their survival. Poor Black men are barred from real jobs, those that pay enough so you can have your own place and support children. Being homeless is becoming normal (60% of the NY shelter population are Black men).

Every year, as the system tightens another notch around their necks, more and more Black children get pushed out of school. In NYC 72% of Black teenage males become high school drop-outs. There was a high school graduation this June where there were 300 girls but only 25 boys. Only thing

is, you get pushed out slickly, in a way that it looks like you're
the quitter, you're the stupid failure.

Last Summer in NYC, 7,000 entering high school students signed up for a City program where they would get
remedial reading classes in the morning and part time paid
jobs in the afternoon. Although all 7,000 got official letters
promising them a job, the Board of Education lied since it
had only proposed to provide half of the students jobs. The
other half were supposed to drop out of the program to prevent drop-outs.

Since the City enrolled the remedial students in June,
but the application deadline for these federally-funded jobs
was in May, there were no jobs at all. Only after TV reporters showed up did Mayor Koch scrape up a few hundred
Summer jobs.

At Bergtraum H.S. out of the 353 students that signed
up only 3 got jobs from the program, despite the City's prom-
ises. Many of the students dropped out in frustration. See,
the program that said it was to prevent drop-outs really was
a psychological warfare behavior-modification program, to
take willing 14 and 15 year olds and condition them into
becoming drop-outs.

And most who do graduate from "Colonial High" find
that their u.s. colonial schooling has been so poor that they
cannot pass the employment tests given at the phone company, the banks and other major corporations. So why not
drop out? And that, too, is supposed to be Black people's
fault.

Coming of age, they learn that survival is illegal. To
get around town you jump the subway tollgates or push thru
the rear doors of buses. On April 15, 1987, all token booth
clerks were counting the number of fare-beaters in a survey.
118,314 people jumped the subway gates that day. At some
stations 40%, 50% or even 70% (the Franklin Park shuttle) of
the riders are illegal.

> *If We say that "crime" is a "reflection of the present state of property relations," then We must also say that for us, these relations are those between a dominated nation and its oppressor and exploiter. The method of economic organization which governs our lives is an imperialist, a neo-colonialist method. Altho this colonial system is structured so as to force many of us to take what We need in order to survive, and altho there are conscious political decisions made by the oppressor, once We find ourselves in the grips of his "criminal justice system," it must also be seen that a conscious political decision must also be made on the part of the colonial subject before his acts can have a subjective, functional political meaning within the context of the national liberation struggle.*
>
> *Put another way: if the "criminal" acts of Afrikans are the results of a "grossly disproportionate distribution of wealth and privilege," which stems from our status as a dominated, neo-colonized nation, then the only way to prevent crime among us is to make a conscious decision to liberate the nation and establish among ourselves a more equitable distribution of wealth and privilege.*
>
> — James Yaki Sayles, "On Transforming the Colonial and 'Criminal' Mentality" from Meditations on Frantz Fanon's Wretched of the Earth: New Afrikan Revolutionary Writings, pp. 81–82.

Since 1982, the transit cops have issued 2,234,659 summons and arrested 51,409 fare-beaters. When you use your girlfriend's food stamps or share her place it's "welfare fraud." Every little thing is illegal in some way, because the system no longer intends for you to survive.

If children see that survival is itself illegal, that they will not even have a place to live, will not have an education, will not have a real job, will not have a family except the streets, then what does it matter? Prison or death at an early age seem normal, and are. "Teenagers consider prison a rite of passage," says Baltimore Mayor Kurt Schmoke. "They come to expect it."

But to be criminalized is to still act within the imperialist system, because you have internalized the values of amerikkka within yourself. You are a colonial criminal instead of a guerrilla. Criminalization channels the instinctive rebellion and need for survival of Black youth back against their own people.

Including back against themselves. It concedes the legitimacy of white authority while breaking its laws.

Colonial criminalization teaches young men, who come of age in a dying community where rules and bonds are disintegrating, that they are and should be "animals." The idea is implanted that they should become lone predators preying on the powerless. The diseased values of the colonial system re-infect their view of the world. The Black Nation may rise, but the existing Black community in amerikkka is dying.

Ya can't understand "Black-on-Black crime" without finally accepting that genocide is a real thing. Anyone with one brain cell still working knows that the cycles of killing and ripping each other off, of children killing themselves with dope and guns, that is overtaking the Black community is not normal crime. It is beyond crime.

You know, the politicians are not the opposites of the drug pusher and the "stickups." They are the role models. Folks are only doing what their mis-leaders and schools and police have always said: do what they tell you to get along, prove how "we" are loyal amerikkkans, get over. So the kid who wants to mug the old lady with her check also says "We oughta bomb Khadaffi's ass!" He eagerly paid his money to watch *Rambo*, cheers on the *Terminator*, carefully checks out *Penthouse* each issue. Amerikkka says hate your own people, kill your brother, make an addict out of your sister, and then kill yourself. And isn't this what's going down?

If you can't escape the amerikkka in your heart, then you can't escape genocide. Time is a thing.

Black men are starting to disappear. In the 1980 census, 14% of the expected Black male population in NYC was missing and went uncounted: dead, in prison, or living anonymously on the streets. *"Black men in New York are more difficult to count than illegal aliens,"* officials said.

But isn't that the point? Afrikans who were colonial subjects now are illegal aliens.

Rates of imprisonment of working age men, 2008

EURO-SETTLER **NEW AFRIKAN** **LATINO**

18- TO 64-YEAR OLDS

1.1% OR 1 IN 87   8% OR 1 IN 12   2.7% OR 1 IN 36

20- TO 34-YEAR OLDS

1.8% OR 1 IN 57   11.4% OR 1 IN 9   3.7% OR 1 IN 37

20- TO 34-YEAR OLDS WITHOUT H.S. DIPLOMA

12% OR 1 IN 8   37.1% OR 1 IN 3   7% OR 1 IN 14

BEN WARD—SMOKE SCREEN

Each year more than 10,000 young Black men ages 15 to 19 are murdered, mostly by each other. That's more deaths than the u.s. military had in Vietnam each year. It was safer to be a GI in Vietnam than it is to be a Black child in the housing projects. And most people still don't want to see that the machinery of genocide has been started up. Someday everyone will see it, but we should see it now.

"Black-on-Black crime" has become the basis for the idea that Black people aren't victimized by white amerikkka but by each other. Ben Ward, the first ever Black NYPD Commissioner, is the lead mouthpiece for this idea, pushing it to more and more outrageous positions all the time (white people love it). At an evening forum of the city association of Black journalists, Ward lashed out:

> And I believe Blacks are victims but we're generally the victims of some other Black committing crimes against us. And the person who burglarizes your house today—when you come home and find there's been a burglary committed, it's probably going to be some young Black who burglarized… and probably going to be some young Black that mugs you on the way home.

Commissioner Ward then defended the routine of white police always shooting down Black men as only natural: "…most of the crime committed in this city is committed by young Black males under 30 years of age. So who are you apt to be shooting at?" After Ward's speech the press made sure to print sympathetic Black comments like these: "'No white person comes into Bedford-Stuyvesant and rapes a grandmother,' said Carlos Russell, a Brooklyn College professor." And reverends lead mothers to the police station to demand more white police protection. A mental smoke screen is created to hide genocide. A paralyzing mental illusion is created, that only the "bad elements" will be killed off, and that the "good elements" are to be saved by amerikkka for the Bill Cosby Show.

This is only clinging to the illusion that the oppressor only wants better behavior and more conformity; an old, old story. Some Indians thought that, desperately clinging to straws. They converted to Christianity to show that they weren't "savages." They promised to help the white soldiers track down "criminal redskins." But at the end were massacred along with their nations. They didn't mind the popular settler saying, "The only good Indian is a dead Indian."

MECHANICS OF GENOCIDE

Genocide amerikkkan-style masks itself as "natural" events and trends. So Black Genocide is not the white stormtroopers machine-gunning the ghetto. Instead, it's the real estate developer shrinking the Black land base. It's the guidance counselor sliding a child out of school. It's the welfare administrator, the mysterious epidemics of infectious diseases, the addicting substances that somehow move from other continents to pop up on the housing project playground, the degrading reservation culture. It's all accidental, all just the way things "naturally" worked out.

And just as the white genocidists signed treaties at every turn with the Indian Nations, each time swearing eternal friendship and to honor Indian rights, so the u.s. government passes Civil Rights acts and swears "Brotherhood" each and every year (genocide is Brother-hood).

The Black land base is shrinking. In New Afrika, the rural South, the white power structure is anticipating the final end of Black farming. "At their peak in 1920, there were 926,000 Black-operated farms..." By 1978 only 57,400 remained.

Black farms are disappearing by 50% every decade. At this rate there will be no Black-operated farms by the end of the century. A Nation of 40 million people will not "legally" have the elemental power to produce one bite of food for their children, or cloth for their clothing, or lumber for their homes.

White experts say that this is only natural, that white farms are failing, also. But Black farmers point to a conspiracy by the u.s. government and the local white power structures. Somehow Black farmers don't get u.s. agriculture dept. crop loans, or get them too late to plant, don't get all those farm subsidies white farmers get. And every time a Black farmer dies the county courthouse crowd tries to force the family to sell out to whites. And most of the time that's what happens.

Like one of our cuter methods. A Black farmer dies, and they don't have a will (because our lawyers discouraged them from making one). Then we rush to find all existing relatives who can possible inherit under our laws. Twenty people show up, some of whom don't even know each other, to get their share of the estate. There is only one farm, and it must be sold under the law to satisfy all the claims. We buy for little money. Divide that among 20 people. Whoopee, they can each buy a new car which will die in three years. But now we have the land, the capital, the ability to produce. Aren't we nice? So helpful.

And in the cities, the Black land base is being gradually hemmed in, shrinking block by block. Black communities are paradoxically the most valuable real estate opportunity in amerikkka. In Boston, the 12 ½ sq. miles of the Black community of Greater Roxbury is the only land adjacent to the downtown biz district that hasn't been "developed." White capitalists plan to spend $750 million buying and gentrifying it, to white-wash Black slums and replace Black housing with "integrated" condos and office buildings.

The City piles extra taxes on Black homeowners (an average of 227% higher than white homeowners in 1984) to put pressure on them to sell. City planners foresee the near total displacement of Roxbury's Black community by the early 21st century. Where will they go? As the American Express television commercial says, *"What will you do?"*

"THEY WANT WHAT WE HAVE"

When Black people don't want to be removed, then they are attacked by white terrorism. In Crown Heights section of Brooklyn, the Hasidic Jewish gangs have been trying to drive Black home-owners out of this once all-Black neighborhood. The home of Willie Mae Reddish and her three sons was firebombed at 1:30 am by two men who ran to hide in the Lubavitcher Hasidic religious school. Police say that they can't find any suspects. Ms. Reddish simply said, "They want what we have." "We allowed them to move in, thinking we could live together," Emeline Nisbet said, "and now they want the whole thing." Ms. Nisbet has been harassed by Hasidic Jews trying to take her home. And Mayor Koch has made a public statement that all the criminals in Crown Heights are Black.

In NYC many sections of Harlem and the South Bronx have lost half to two-thirds of their Black populations. Fifteen years of landlord arsons and City tax delinquency take-overs have emptied whole blocks (the City owns 60% of all Harlem buildings), either to shelve them for future middle-class gentrification or to simply reduce Black housing. On the West Side, yuppie condominiums have already pushed over ten blocks into what used to be the border of Black Harlem.

i mean, Blacks and Latinos formerly occupied one-third of all the land in Manhattan, where today white yuppies are paying $800-$1,000 per room in rent, where it costs $100,000 to buy a studio condominium. Try and guess what one-third of Manhattan is worth. Billions? And that's just one city. As with the Indian Nations, displacing Black people from the land is not an expense for amerikkka, but a windfall of immense profits.

Black urban communities have been gutted by "integration." What is common is the wiping out of Black shops, restaurants, skilled trades, and small businesses that were the service infrastructure of the old Black community. In Miami, the Black community of 250,000 had at the time of the 1980 Liberty City uprising, only two clothing stores and one hardware store owned by Black people. Yet, Liberty City was once a more complete and thriving community.

> *When the racial barriers went down [in the late 1960s],*
> *Blacks poured into the white stores, restaurants, ho-*
> *tels—devastating the Black-run economy almost overnight.*
> *Overtown, a section once called the "Harlem of the South,"*
> *used to play host to Sarah Vaughan and Duke Ellington;*
> *the dining room of its Sir John Hotel provided linen*

tablecloth and silver. Today, Overtown is a ghost city; its stores are abandoned and its streets populated by junkies and stray dogs.

Black people have been systematically starved out of Miami's economy. Black factory workers were 10.3% of the Miami Black community in 1968, but only 2.2% in 1978 after a decade of "integration."

In 1960, Black people owned 25% of all Miami gas stations, but by 1979 owned only 9%. Cubans had taken over the other 18% of Miami gas stations formerly owned by Black people. This change was government policy.

In those years, 1968 to 1979, the Small Business Administration in Miami loaned an equal $47 million to Cubans and $47 million to whites, but only $6.4 million to Black small businesses. Black women are not even being hired as cleaning staff in the resort hotels anymore. As a final touch, urban renewal placed huge new expressways around the border of the Black community, physically blocking them off from downtown Miami. It looks like a military plan. From a community to a reservation in less than twenty years.

Land, a stable territory, is the basis of nationhood. It is the basis of community, without which there is no real independence or economy. So when amerikkka begins a program, North as well as South, urban as well as rural, to dispossess Black people from their territory and remove them into nowhere, it signals that what was done to the Indian Nations is now planned for the Black Nation.

Black people with education are still needed for white-collar jobs, but already for the bottom half, the Black underclass, there is no longer a place for them inside north amerikkka outside the reservation (projects, shelters, prisons). Like the Indians before them, the Black underclass are becoming nomads and squatters, homeless. They are dying.

Everything that kills Black people is encouraged. Drug addiction is the clearest example. Everyone knows that heroin and cocaine are killing Black people more efficiently than firing squads could. Drugs are getting Black children to kill each other. And everyone also knows that all this is coming from somewhere else. i mean, Black people aren't growing any dope plants in jungles, they're not flying airplanes full of it across oceans, they're not the folks with badges and guns who enforce things, so it's got to be coming from someone else.

AND SHOOT UP THE BLACK NATION, TOO

Drug addiction in the Black community is really a u.s. government program, a counter-insurgency project run by the Central Intelligence Agency. The CIA has always supplied most of the hard drugs for the ghetto dope traffic, while local police supply protection for the big pushers. This is a fact. It's an unreported news story smoldering away in the back of the white closet.

As the Yankee traders did with the opium traffic in 19th century China, the CIA has left the stateside distribution and street sales of the drugs to local "natives." It controls the source, the production. In doing so it kills two birds with one stone. For the CIA has used Black and Latino drug sales to finance its covert wars in Asia and Central Amerika.

While the u.s. military was busy invading Vietnam in the 1960s, the CIA itself was having to operate and finance several other Asian wars all by itself. In the neighboring country of Laos, the CIA had formed what it named "The Secret Army" out of 15,000 mercenaries (mostly Meo tribesmen led by General Vang Pao). Their task was to destabilize the shaky Lao neutralist government, and replace it with one of CIA employees. In neutral Burma, the CIA was sponsoring yet another war, this time by the 20,000 soldier "Shan State Army." It was a right-wing Christian ethnic insurgency. There as well the goal was to install a CIA led government.

Financing wars is very expensive, even for amerikkka. So the u.s. government turned to Southeast Asia heroin trafficking to help pay for its dirty wars in the Third World. CIA airplanes from the front company Air America flew into the jungles with guns and flew out with dope. Most of the heroin used in the Black community comes from CIA sources, the deadly profits used to feed and pay salaries for secret Asian armies. And shoot up the Black Nation, too. There was a sixties saying: "Uncle Sam is the pusher man." In the Sixties the Black community found itself flooded with new supplies of high-grade heroin from Asia, supplied by the CIA's Asian armies, at the same time that thousands of Black GIs were coming home addicted. In 'Nam, drugs were cheap, easy to get, all but legal. The CIA was preparing its future market at home.

Now, the CIA has taught the heroin trade to its latest pupils, the Afghan Islamic rebels. They now supply most of the heroin used by Black addicts. These are the same men that Ronnie says are "freedom fighters," who rebelled against the pro-Russian government when it recognized Afghan women's right of divorce.

CIA-AFGHAN REBELS THE SOURCE

A *NY Times* report from Afghan rebel-held territory admitted
the role of the drug trade:

> *In the shade of an ancient tree to the side of a field where
> the farmers worked in Musa Qala, an Islamic teacher
> explained the importance of opium to the rebels. [opium
> from poppy plants is made into heroin]*

> *"How else can we get money?" said the teacher, an elderly
> man named Mohammed Rasul with a thick gray-and-
> black beard and large, watery eyes. His brother, Nazim
> Akunzada, is regarded by other rebels as the most power-
> ful commander in the Helmand Province. They say his
> family has large land holdings that include extensive
> poppy fields.*

> *"We must grow and sell opium to fight our Holy War
> against the Russian nonbelievers," Mr. Rasul said.
> Comments like these were heard from dozens of rebels
> throughout the journey...*

> *International anti-narcotics officials in Pakistan say
> they believe that Afghanistan is the largest single source
> of illicit opium... A State Department report in February
> described Afghanistan and the bordering tribal areas of
> Pakistan as "the world's leading source of illicit heroin
> exports to the United States and Europe."*

Straight from the CIA to the housing project playground.

And the u.s. government, which gives the dope grow-
ers their guns and is their connect to the outside world, it
doesn't know what's going on? Give us a break. They plan for
Malcolm's grandchildren to be junkies.

You can stuff all that "freedom fighter," "Islamic Holy
War," blah blah. These are just more sick men with their sick

religions, who want to keep women enslaved and get over selling dope. That's why they and Ronnie get it on.

And in NYC the NYPD has been the muscle protecting the ghetto dope traffic, particularly protecting the cocaine distribution until it got firmly rooted. Oh, they make their usual number of busts, and sooner or later everyone Black on the street gets busted, but never interfering with the dope system itself. Everything that kills Black people is encouraged.

BEN ADMITS GUILT

This is heavy but it's not a paranoid thing, it's a fact. There's a good source for it–Police Commissioner Ben Ward himself. When Ward was speaking before the association of Black journalists this year, he was getting hot under the collar as his flunky remarks brought choruses of boos and hisses. Finally, Ben lost his cool and blurted out:

> *I don't think you can just stand and hiss and complain as we hear it here… I am catching more hell from you than McGuire [former commissioner] ever caught from any of you* **and McGuire allowed 800, 800 storefront drugstores to be opened in this city and not a damn thing was done about narcotics enforcement for six years!**

Check that out. The police knew about the dope parlors opening up in the Black and Latino communities, even kept a count of them. But the police commissioner gave orders to let them alone. That's what they say. If we can't see what that means we'd better get retreaded. But when Black people try and stop drug dealers, which means with force, then police wake up and arrest those opposing the pushers. Is that a co-incidence, or a program?

Black drug addiction is not an "uncontrolled epidemic," as some say. It is very controlled. It is u.s. chemical-bacteriological warfare towards Black Genocide. It's so open, so pervasive in the Black community as misery and the need to feel good chemically get deeper, that it has de facto become semi-legalized and normal.

Some people in the system say they might as well go all the way and formalize things, legalizing heroin and cocaine sales to Black people. Baltimore Mayor Kurt Schmoke, who is the former states attorney and is on the u.s. justice department's "Committee on Research on Law Enforcement," has called for a study on de-criminalizing drugs (kids could buy crack at the corner grocery store):

> *My sense is that if we decriminalize it, one impact would be to drop the bottom out of the market. The cost of drugs would drop, and, one hopes, related crime, including murder.*

However, the CIA doesn't want to "drop the bottom out of the market," or to reduce Black crime, especially Blacks killing Blacks. And no one is going to arrest the ruling class, after all. But the discussion of legalizing hard drug sales to Black people, formally or informally, shows how the system is getting people to accept the mass addiction of Black youth as normal.

Notice that the drug epidemic has intersected and combined with the AIDS epidemic? More coincidences. You heard about so-called designer drugs? Well, AIDS is like a designer disease. An incurable disease that comes out of no-where, with no known origin, and that targets gay men, drug addicts, Afrikans and Latinos. Just who amerikkka wants to get rid of.

AIDS COVERUP

Around the world most folks think that AIDS is a man-made virus secretly developed as a CBW (chemical-bacteriological warfare) weapon by the u.s. military. And that it got loose while being secretly tested on Afrikans. You know that's exactly who they'd test it on. A series by the *Washington Afro-American* kept finding that answer to where AIDS came from:

> *It is the theory of one local geneticist, who does not want to be identified in this piece, that the AIDS virus could have resulted from a major flaw in the manipulation of a virus.*
>
> *And he pointed to the medical and military communities reluctance to probe this obvious possibility and simple explanation for the spread of AIDS as a clear indication of a "cover up."*

The Afro-American noted that in 1950 the u.s. army secretly sprayed the bacteria *serratia marcescens* from airplanes over San Francisco. The germ was supposed to cause mild respiratory ailments, like a cold, which from local doctors' reports would allow the military to measure how effective its aerial spraying techniques were. The u.s. later had to admit that *serratia marcescens* was an "opportunistic" infection which could

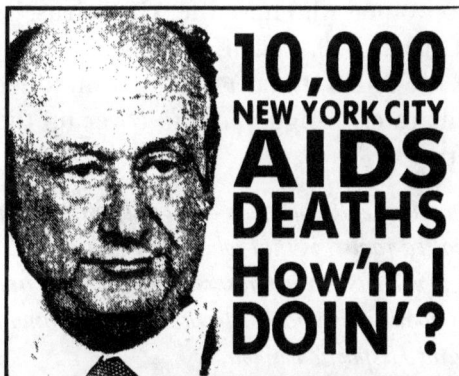

10,000 NEW YORK CITY AIDS DEATHS How'm I DOIN'?

produce fatal respiratory problems in already ill or weakened patients. A small number of Black victims did die.

In 1951 the navy coated the outside of ten wooden cargo containers with bacteria in another secret CBW test. The experiment was to see how the bacteria would be transmitted to men unwittingly handling the boxes at a Pennsylvania supply depot. A report on the test said:

> *Of the three infectious bacteria, aspergilus fumigatis had been specifically chosen because Black workers at the base would be particularly susceptible to it.*

Throughout the 1950s and 1960s, the u.s. military secretly tested many CBW agents on unknowing Afrikans, both in the u.s. and overseas (such as in Savannah, Georgia and in the Bahamas), before promising congress that any such experiments would be banned. But medical researchers now believe that remote Central Afrikan villages had AIDS back in the 1950s, but were wiped out in isolation and no one in the West ever heard about it. Could AIDS be an old experiment in genocide that eventually escaped the testing grounds? Or is it a new genetic weapon of imperialist science to reshape society?

What is certain is that AIDS is going to savage the Black community. In New York City as of mid-1987 there are already 50,000 women who have the AIDS virus, 80% of them Black and Latina. B.D. Colen, *Newsday* science editor, has written that the AIDS threat to straight middle-class whites is being deliberately exaggerated to cover up the specificity of the target:

> *When public health officials don't tell you, for fear of being called racist, is that when they talk about the dramatic increase in heterosexual AIDS, they are really talking about a dramatic increase in AIDS among poor Black and Hispanic women.*

BLANK IDENTITY

The United Nations definition of genocide includes not only the physical extermination of a nation or people, but also the death of their culture. Biological survival of individuals or families is not necessarily survival of a people or nation. Without their culture, which is their distinctive way of life, their language and traditions, their own way of interacting with nature, a people as such no longer exist.

Also, culture is a survival mechanism, and without it a people cannot defend themselves. The ruling class understood this when they set up the Indian reservation system in the 1870s, which pretended to "protect" Indians by confining them to areas of land too small or barren to sustain their old way of life. These were the first u.s. housing projects, the first Welfare system. And then Indian children were to be "saved" by being sent away to bureau of indian affairs boarding schools off the reservation. This was not voluntary. Selected children were just physically taken.

Many thousands of Indian children were tortured for years in these behavior modification prisons, which were upfront intended to de-Indianize them, to wipe out all Indian culture in their minds. Children had to wear white clothing, follow white middle-class rules and customs, speak only u.s. English. Any time a child spoke in their native tongue they were hit. They were kept isolated from their families. Many children were destroyed.

The plan was to gradually manufacture generations of imprisoned "colorless" people who would not be Indian. Who wouldn't know what Indians knew or think as Indians thought. Despite successful Indian children's resistance (another untold story), the u.s. government stubbornly persisted in this reach for cultural genocide of Indian children until the stormy 1960s (now they've only changed tactics). Genocide begins with the children.

A mother who pleaded guilty to fraudulently enrolling her six-year-old son in the wrong school district has been sentenced to five years in prison. Tonya McDowell sent her son to an elementary school in Norwalk, Connecticut, instead of her home city of Bridgeport. The 34-year-old, who was homeless when she was charged with felony larceny last year, said she wanted the best education possible for the boy.

ULTIMATE SEXUAL CRIMINALS

Not the serial rapist or the child rapist, but the Black woman who dares to control her life, the lives of her children, and the life of her Nation. This is the ultimate sexual crime in a world dominated by Euro-imperialism.

Here in 1987, Daniel Patrick Moynihan is once again the cats-paw, leading the social-engineering necessary for genocide. But what Moynihan is saying today is not what he was saying in the Sixties. So there is Moynihan I and Moynihan II. Now, Moynihan and the ruling class aren't saying one word about any jobs for Black men, or about racism. The whole problem, according to Moynihanism, is that shiftless welfare mothers don't want to work and support their children. So amerikkka has to discipline them. White man's discipline.

Mayor Koch has gone on television with his snide, insulting pleas for welfare mothers to go get a job: "Work is good for you. Try it, you'll really like it." As if it was their choice. Moynihan is attacking them in print as women who are so sick that they have *neither* a job nor a husband:

> *Imagine a state with a population one quarter larger than Delaware's. Almost a quarter million families (241,000) live in this state, but there are no adult males. The adult males live somewhere else; where else no one is quite sure... In these circumstances, the female heads of these families are forced to look for work. However, of the nearly quarter million such women, only about 6,300 have found work, and most of the jobs are part-time.*

> *Shall we call this state Delaware on Hudson? For the population described above lives in New York City. It is called the welfare population.*

> *What exotic pattern of in-migration, out-migration, social expectation turned upside down, economic ruin, social disaster, and now, finally, plague have brought about this society without fathers?*

Moynihan is upfront in saying that mothers with young children could work if they really wanted to, so he wants to force them.

> *What we allowed, in Goodman's words, was for parents to "walk out on their kids' lives, letting them slide down the economic chute." ... Where some 72 percent of women with children are in the work force (54% of women with children under age 6), less than 5 percent of welfare recipients are in the work force.*

Just like Black men, Black women of the underclass are being criminalized, too. As sexual criminals, who are having children against white orders, who are defending their children when amerikkka wants them to die.

TAKING BLACK CHILDREN AWAY

Black women are being slammed as sluts, drug addicts, unfit mothers, sexual criminals. 'Cause if you want to commit genocide that's where you got to strike. You've got to neutralize Black women as women, eradicate them. You've gotta drive them out of housing, nuke them with male violence, flood them with crack, all as a pretext to take their children. You've got to separate Black women from their children, and demand that they stop having children. Only, you got to say it's all just your liberal concern for the poor.

This is the new attack of Moynihan and Moynihan-ism.

Moynihan is sponsoring a welfare reform act which is only a pretext to force more Black children into the hands of white men. His "Family Security Act" would force welfare mothers to take either low-wage jobs or no-wage work for local government. Being an unpaid clerk at the welfare office or mopping the floor at the daycare center. Or else. There's a "historic bipartisan consensus" on this kind of plan in some form.

"Workfare" it's misnamed. But it isn't about work. It's about smashing Black and Latina women apart from their kids. It's so disruptive, so out there and extreme, that some welfare agencies are themselves protesting to the media:

> *Megan E. McLaughlin, executive vice-president of the Federation of Protestant Welfare Agencies, complained that when benefits are cut to mothers who do meet work requirements, they cannot provide for their families and are at risk of having their children placed in foster care...* **"Senator Moynihan's bill goes beyond benign neglect. It is a deliberate plan to remove children from families that he considers unworthy..."**

Hey, what they're saying is that there really is a conspiracy, in the highest levels of the government, to kidnap hundreds of thousands more Black children. To target and destroy Black families led by women.

When Dick says "welfare reform," "job counseling," what it's really going to play out to in the end is desperate women trying to hold that low-wage or no-wage job while taking care of kids in the shelters, in welfare hotels. Doubling and tripling up in rooms in disappearing slums. Praying that you don't get sick. Praying that you don't lose your job because your kids get sick and have to wait for hours at the clinic. It means being squeezed off welfare, losing that job, and not getting back on unless you give up your children to foster care ("It's for their own good!").

Moynihan's "Family Security Act" reads: "Would require that all recipients of cash assistance with children age 3 or older (with state option to drop the age to 1) participate, at State direction, in the JOBS program."

Of course, adequate childcare won't be provided for most kids. And if you get laid off or lose your apartment, or if you get ill, then you'll lose custody of your children because under the "reform" you won't really be permitted to get back on welfare with them. It's a one-way trip.

Before, when the ruling class wanted lots of Black labor, Black women were told to have large families, husbands or no. The slavemaster would rape Afrikan women to get more slave children. When Black labor was needed in Southern agriculture and Northern factories, Black women were expected to raise many children. But now that the patriarchal ruling class wants to erase the Color Black from north amerikkka, now they say it's immoral and wrong for Black women to have children, since they can't support them. Or, to be more precise, since white amerikkka doesn't want Black women to support them. But it's not about labor or money, anymore.

And all the while the power structure is pressuring, squeezing. Cutting back Black employment on the one hand while on the other making welfare less and less livable. In

NYC, between 1970 and 1986, the aid to dependent children benefits of the average welfare family were actually cut 38%. And no one in government is proposing to raise this.

What they're saying is that white economics must rule Black women's sexuality, the nature of the Black family, and whether the Black population grows or declines. As though they were cattle. But it's not about economics, it's about disarming the Black Nation. They don't want Black women to raise Black warriors and Black amazons. They want less and less Black people.

Propaganda for their fantasy nuclear family is only the lever for tighter government control of women's bodies and women's lives. In the 1960s, Moynihan hoped that u.s. imperialism could use Black men to control Black women. They've given up on that. Now, they see that white men have to directly impose control over Black women.

To do this the patriarchal ruling class has called in all their helpers. Not only Ronnie and Moynihan and Mayor Crazy Ed, but the white women's movement and the puppet Black middle-class men. Everyone is in on the attack against Black women. From all angles, on all fronts.

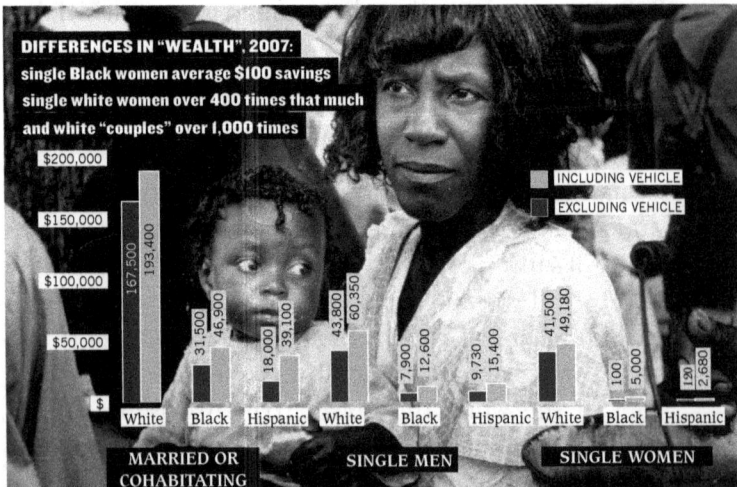

DIFFERENCES IN "WEALTH", 2007:
single Black women average $100 savings
single white women over 400 times that much
and white "couples" over 1,000 times

INCLUDING VEHICLE
EXCLUDING VEHICLE

	MARRIED OR COHABITATING			SINGLE MEN			SINGLE WOMEN		
	White	Black	Hispanic	White	Black	Hispanic	White	Black	Hispanic
Including vehicle	167,500	31,500	18,000	43,800	7,900	9,730	41,500	100	190
Excluding vehicle	193,400	46,900	39,100	60,350	12,600	15,400	49,180	5,000	2,680

GENOCIDE NEEDS BLACK SEXISM

In the Black community there have always been sexist voices supporting Moynihan-ism. Back in the 1970s the cry for male supremacy was so loudly intertwined with Black Power politics that even many Black women intellectuals, like sociologist Joyce Ladner, felt compelled to agree:

> The bold assertion of Black masculinity has required that Black women redefine their roles… The "traditional strong" Black woman has probably outlived her usefulness because this role has been challenged by the Black man.

Many middle-class Black leaders openly hold that Black women must be subordinate, and should not have families without a man to run things. Robert Staples put this on front street, not in *Hustler* or *Penthouse* where it belongs, but in the pages of *Black Scholar*, a prestigious academic journal:

> That Black men are not staying with their families is due to a confluence of certain factors, not the least among them is the fact that some women make the decisions and desertion is his form of masculine protest… Desertion, moreover, is the lower-class male's style of exercising his masculine perquisite.

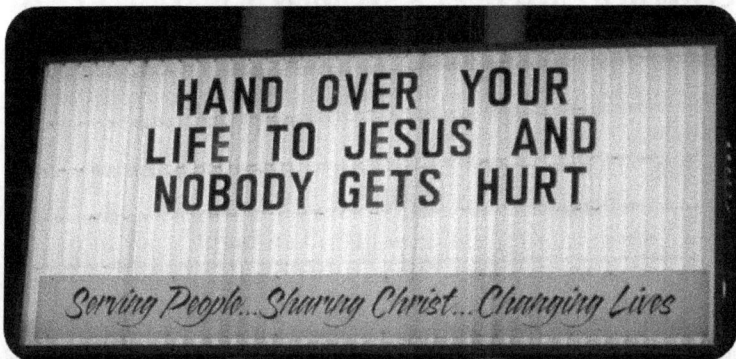

HAND OVER YOUR LIFE TO JESUS AND NOBODY GETS HURT

Serving People… Sharing Christ… Changing Lives

To Black sociologist Robert Staples, for Black men to desert their children is the "masculine" thing to do, just asserting yourself. While Black women shouldn't be strong or independent—"femininity" is defined as being submissive and white as can be. Sexism and Black Genocide go together as the old saying sez, like a horse and carriage. *Black Scholar* prints this stuff not because they're necessarily defending it, but because it typifies a major point of view in the community.

> *The middle-class Black male, with a wider range of choices, screens out the strong Black woman beforehand in his choice of mates. Anyone who has met the typical middle-class Black wife knows she scores higher on the "femininity" scale than her unmarried counterpart. Some middle-class Black men turn to white women who fit even better the model of femininity as set forth in this country....*

> *Is this sexism? I guess so. It is, also, a matter of personal choice that cannot be denied men. They have the right to choose a woman that meets their perceived needs, even if their exercise of that right limits the life options of women...*

CONTROLLING BLACK WOMEN'S SEXUALITY

That same sexism is being directed by the patriarchal ruling class in its campaign to stop Black women from having babies. Even tho Black women, married and single alike, are having less babies now than at any time in u.s. history. Even tho there are less Black babies on welfare in 1987 than there were 15 years ago. "Less" is not good enough for white people. None, zero, zip, da nada, is their real goal for Black children.

And it isn't about giving Black women the right to control their own bodies, either. That right is a life-giving thing, and every mother wants her daughter to escape (you know what i mean), but what masks itself as "population planning," "pro-family values," "unwed mothers crisis," and blah and so forth, is just a campaign to place tighter white male controls on Black women's sexuality.

Look at the ridiculous scandal and fury this Summer over Liz Walker's pregnancy. Thirty-six years old, single, and earning a good living, Walker decided that she couldn't wait any longer to have a baby. So what? What made it a big deal is that she is the first Black news co-anchor at Boston's WBZ-TV. No one could say that Liz Walker couldn't support her baby, or that she's an unfit parent. What they did say was that as a role model, she had given up her right to have a child without a husband.

All the middle-class sexists white and Black alike were trashing her. "We are trying to create proper values, this is precisely the wrong kind of signal to send," said Rev. Earl Jackson of Roxbury Baptist Church. "What she's doing is wrong." Dr. James Comer, head of child psychiatry at Yale University, told the press that he was "disappointed" in Liz Walker.

Syndicated columnist Carl Rowan attacked Liz Walker's pregnancy in print as "destructive," and added: "What we have is a national social tragedy." To them any more Black babies is a crisis. While being a "role model" means to follow white men's orders down into Black Genocide.

"If they weren't so overpopulated, they wouldn't need so much space"

WE DON'T LIKE THEIR LOOKS, SO...

Now that Black Genocide is underway, corporations are getting more relaxed, saying that poor Black women won't get hired because of their looks. Yes, we've gotten so cocky about killing Black women and children off that businesses don't have to use those tired-out lies any more. (You know: "I'd really love to hire you, but we need someone with computer background who speaks nine European languages and has five years experience in aerospace engineering, sorry.")

Ms. Susan Purser, an official with a Boston job retraining program, says that one of her Black trainees has a good chance under corporate hiring rules:

> *I think I can place her easily. She's thin, she looks good and she does not have that street language that often goes against Blacks.*

If white men don't like the way you look or the way you talk, then you have no right to feed your family, no right to live.

Ms. Purser says that the current business thinking about hiring poor Black women is: "You have to look good, be able to spell, not be too fat, have all your teeth – and all that for $5 an hour."

Black women of the underclass will never have regular employment, concedes Samuel Ehrenhalt, federal bureau of labor statistics regional commissioner in NYC: "The problem is single mothers in poverty, Mr. Ehrenhalt said. 'The circumstances under which these mothers would enter the labor force seem very remote,' he said."

If poor Black women are supposed to get off welfare, but should not expect real jobs, isn't that the same message amerikkka gave to the Indian Nations? The program is not survival but death, dying out.

Since they are women, as a final insult, the ruling class puts out that it's all their fault, that it's just because poor

Black women *look wrong*, aren't attractive enough to live. "Yes, boss, you're right," say the Robert Staples and the other puppet Black middle-class men. Criminalizing Black women has become a career for more than just Daniel Patrick Moynihan in this Land of Equal Opportunity.

WHERE ARE WHITE WOMEN?

And white women, where are we in all this? It's hard to find us. The so-called women's movement says, "we don't have the same program as Ronnie"–but they do. Only on the second front of attack, around the back. What position do you expect from the patriarchy? Still, women are the key. You have to separate Black women from Black children. And you've got to convince white women that it's not an attack on women, that it's ok.

NOW isn't a women's movement but is the patriarchy's program for women. Just the same as the German middle-class feminists of the 1930s, who decided to work for equality with Nazi men within the genocide system. Genocide, those

German feminists said, was not a woman's issue. And Jewish women were not really women to them, just as Black women at the Martinique Hotel aren't really women to us.

If Euro-amerikkkan women wanna be something different than Dicks without pricks, then we'd better turn our backs (or guns) on the drive for full equality within Dick's house. Because it is a slaughterhouse with us as the butchers.

We siphon off just enough Black political women to use as ammunition for our battles for privilege, or as sprinkles to make us feel better while we do our white thing. We pull from the New Afrikan Nation, from the Black community, just enough to nourish us. But we put nothing back. Not one drop of our sweat or our blood.

Genocide, after all, is not a "women's issue." Not for Dick's women, anyway.

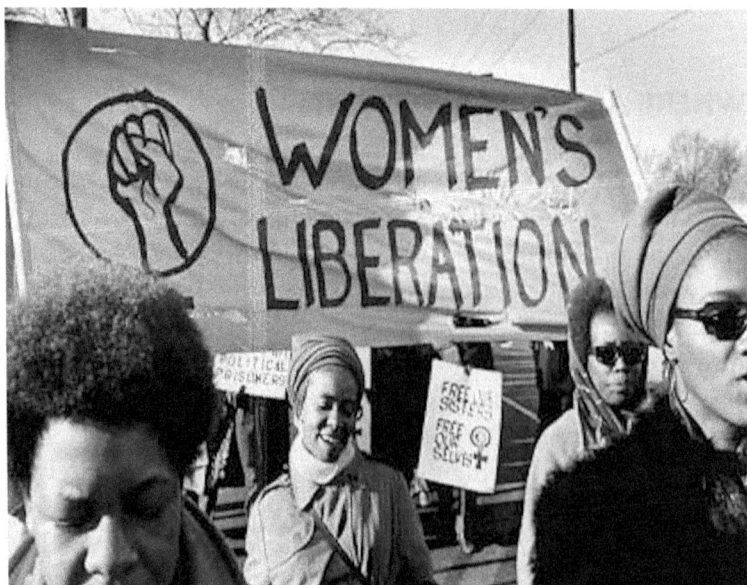

THE IDEA OF LIBERATION
CAME FROM THE BLACK NATION

The media loved to picture women's liberation as a freaky white thing, but the facts show differently. In 1972, Louis Harris-Virginia Slims opinion polls revealed that while only a 35% minority of white women expressed "sympathy with efforts of women's liberation groups," a 67% majority of Black women polled identified with the statement.

Radical women's organizing found thousands of receptive minds at the end of the 1960s. Women's liberation was irresistible, an "idea whose time has come." And in the beginning it was explicitly revolutionary, trying to link rebellious white women up with the Third World. The most popular political poster on college dormitory room walls was the famous one of the young Vietnamese woman guerrilla holding a rifle.

At the June 1967 national conference of Students for a Democratic Society (SDS), the main white student antiwar group of the Sixties, the women's liberation workshop explored the relationship between themselves and the Third World:

> As we analyze the position of women in capitalist society and especially in the United States we find that women are in a colonial relationship to men and we recognize ourselves as part of the Third World... Women, because of their colonial relationship to men, have to fight for their own independence. This fight for our own independence will lend to the growth and development of the revolutionary movement in this country.

This, as we now know, didn't see how deep women's colonialization really is. Women have a colonial relationship to men, but white women are not part of the Third World. For white women live the contradiction of being oppressed and also

being the oppressor, being aggressed upon and yet being aggressors, having white privileges without having white power.
If we think about it, what could be more colonized than for
women to join in men's crimes?

This brings us back to the relationship between Black
Genocide and the women's movement for white equality.

If the just-starting women's liberation movement had
survived it would have divided white society, and would have
seriously endangered the plans for Black Genocide. Born
out of the sparks from Black Liberation, with its own revolutionary pulse, women's liberation would have been a guerrilla movement behind enemy lines. It might have sabotaged
the machinery of genocide. Just as the student antiwar movement did to the invasion of Vietnam. Once was more than
enough for amerikkka's ruling class. Black Genocide and, indeed, stabilizing the white home base, required dealing with
the new women's liberation movement.

NEO-COLONIALIZING WOMEN

The power structure neutralized women's liberation by smothering it under the "neutra-sweet" women's movement for white equality. And then pretended that they were both the same thing. The latter movement is more like a u.s. government social-engineering program than a real movement.

Tuning into the dissatisfaction that white middle-class women had, the u.s. ruling class had even earlier encouraged them to escape being only housewives, and promised them some of the economic and social advantages that their white brothers and husbands had.

Years before there was any white women's struggle, any protests, any organizations, the ruling class was urging white women to have "Civil Rights" of their own. In 1960, the problem of the "trapped housewife" was promoted by the media, with stories in *Time, Newsweek, Redbook, Good Housekeeping, Harpers Bazaar,* and on a CBS Television Report.

President John F. Kennedy set up a President's Commission on the Status of Women in December 1961, and many governors followed by setting up state commissions on

women. All without any militant white women's protests, or even mass civil disobedience, as had taken place during the much earlier Women's Suffrage movement. The initiative was coming down from the power structure.

The 1963 Civil Rights Act contained a clause, Title VII, which not only prohibited discrimination by race, color, religion, and national origin, but also on the basis of sex. That same year Betty Friedan's *Feminine Mystique* was published and became a bestseller. Its main thrust was on middle-class white women's right to escape the "comfortable concentration camp" of housewifery, and to pursue careers alongside her white husband.

Finally, the National Organization of Women–NOW–was founded on October 26, 1965, by white women attending a Washington DC luncheon for members of official state women's commissions. From the start its main purpose was to pass better legislation for white equality. As Betty Friedan scrawled on a paper napkin at the luncheon: "full equality for women in a fully equal partnership with men." NOW is still the only national women's organization, an "umbrella group" with some 150,000 members, 765 chapters, offices and paid staff.

NOW was a counter-insurgency operation against sisterhood, keeping discontented white women loyal to the white male power. Officially designated women role models (they aren't leaders because white women have no leaders of our own) say getting accepted by the system, the male system, is where it's at.

Ms. magazine's socialite editor, said this year:

> There's much more activity on campuses now than in the '60s and 70s. We're used to thinking about campus activism in male ways, such as rioting and burning buildings. We're also used to thinking of a radical as somebody who drops out. For women, it's more radical to drop in.

And yet NOW is not the problem. The male-sanctioned movement for white equality is a natural thing in this society, and was always going to be here. Its uncontested success comes from the contradiction in the radical feminism of the 1970s. That was much more the problem. Radical feminists believed in the unity of white women just as much as their liberal sisters did. While sisterhood demands the dis-unity of white women.

What white women have united behind is getting more money for themselves, to put it bluntly. Their own economic advancement is the only common ground that liberals and radical feminists, marriage reformers and lesbian separatists, can agree upon. Sisterhood demands the dis-unity of white women. Demands that women who want to find a way of life without colonialism, whatever the price, break away from those women who intend to profit from colonialism. And i mean colonialism in all senses of the word.

Women's liberation was lost because feminists wanted to separate somewhat from white men while still dining at the same long table. Jane didn't want to share Dick's bed and certainly didn't want to pick up after him, but she was hooked on the goodies in Dick's house. Jane wanted to be Dick's favorite sister, with a little room of her own in his big white house. Despite its great breakthrough, radical feminism lost direction because it wasn't radical enough about colonialization.

Without any wars, without any Mississippis, middle-class white women were handed the economic advancement they wanted. Capitalism wanted them to have it. Black women had once demanded the right to eat at the lunch counter, but white women wanted to own the restaurant. And now they do.

Mary King is a good example of this new equality for white women. Growing up in New York as the daughter of a Southern Methodist minister, she left college to join the southern Civil Rights movement. By 1964 Mary King had taken major responsibilities for communications and press relations at SNCC headquarters.

When she and other white women were forced out by the tide of Black Power in 1965, she was bitter: "I was terribly disappointed for a long time... I was most affected by the way that the Black women turned against me. That hurt more than the guys." She turned to liberal women's consciousness raising.

In the new climate, the Mary Kings were welcomed back into the white clan. When the Carter Administration took over Washington in 1976, King became assistant director of the VISTA program. She married Dr. Peter Bourne, President Carter's advisor on drug abuse. Bourne became famous for helping to popularize cocaine use, declaring to the press that it was a non-addicting recreational drug. Last heard of, Mary King was the executive director of a council for u.s. investment in the Arab world. Middle-class white women have come a long way, indeed. All the way back home.

On the 20th anniversary of the founding of NOW, Betty Friedan accurately said: "NOW went beyond our wildest dreams. Our daughters take it for granted that they will play in the Little League, that they can be astronauts and that they can run for President. It broke through the barriers of explicit sex discrimination."

Because that's the way the power structure wanted it.

WHITE EQUALITY EQUALS BLACK GENOCIDE

White men didn't like this, but the government and corporations forced it on them. Without a vote, either. Irregardless of what men feel, the system needed white women's role to change for a series of related reasons. In the era of government-controlled Civil Rights, white women have been designated as the largest "minority." Thus, white people are both the majority and the "minority" that needs special consideration. Black people have suggested that while they are sympathetic to white women's need for jobs and income, the whole thing looks like a con game. Welcome to amerikkka!

Check it out: In the 13 equal opportunity years before Ronnie, from 1966 to 1979, the total Black share of all professional jobs rose to only 4.1%. And a disproportionate share of those Black professionals are poorly-paid schoolteachers and caseworkers.

In sharp contrast, during those 13 years the share of all professional jobs held by white women zoomed from 13% to 31.6%. So that in 1966 whites held 96.5% of all professional jobs, but 13 years of equal opportunity later the total white share was still 90.5%.

White women are, in fact, the main economic beneficiaries of Civil Rights. "'Educated white women are really members of the family,' said Dr. Phyllis A. Wallace, a professor at the Sloan School of Management at MIT, who serves on corporate boards." The family of man.

White unity is what it's all about. The ruling class needs and is getting a unified white society to carry out Black Genocide. Unlike the mess it got into over the Vietnam War. White women were given a stake in the system to control them. White women are owning more real estate, more land, more small businesses, make up over half the students at many law schools, are becoming government officials and doctors, executives and military officers.

Naturally, the command centers of this patriarchal society are closed to them, since the top circle of business and government will always be the Men's Room. But white women have come so far, so fast, that they are proud just to be junior partners at the bottom of the patriarchy. Too bad all those Black women and children have to die, they think, but look at all the real estate it opens up. White women missed out on the land-grab when the Indian Nations were wiped out and reservationized back in the 18th and 19th centuries, so they're determined not to be left out of the new looting as Black people are reservationized and exterminated.

White women's equality is only another name for Black Genocide. 'Cause the real question in equality is, equal to what?

WITH DICK'S GOODIES COMES DICK

Only, how come there's more and more male violence of all kinds against women here? Sexual harassment and rape is amerikkka's amateur sport. Serial murder? We've become numb, used to it. Violence against women is men's mass movement. They had to have one of their own, you know.

Because this is white unity, too. This is the flip side of the coin. White equality has two sides. Black Genocide is one, and mass violence against women is the other. And the so-called women's movement can deal with neither problem, can't even confront the two problems.

The ruling class needs white men to be white men, to be their violent, racist, greedy, immoral, self-centered and manipulatible selves. So it has to let them, threatened and angry as they are over women's existence, take it out on women and children in an increasing frenzy of hatred.

Don't fool ourselves. There is no end in sight, you know,

until women end it. This is white unity, too. This is what the
system lets white men do. If you're a white woman you can
get your own American Express card, but men get to rape
you if they want to. Fair is fair, in the family of man.

And the women's movement for white equality, what of
it there is, is paralyzed like a bunny staring at a snake and
can't do anything. In fact, they don't even want to think too
much about male violence. They wanna think about their fav
subject, more money.

i mean, this is the heart of the beast. Without which
capitalism or any other oppressive system could not live. For
5,000 years men have held women and children as property,
to be used, sold, bought, exploited, raped, beaten and killed
as they wanted to. All the institutions of male civilization,
most certainly including all religion and the nuclear family,
reinforce this. Do you think men can be made non-danger-
ous with a law, a speech, a little psychology, that 5,000 years
of habitual sickness can be wished away? This is it, the heart
of the beast, what it's all about.

Like Black Genocide, male violence against women can
only be stopped with a 9mm, with political-military methods.
Only Amazons can protect women. And there is increasingly
no safety in this world, only a choice of what future to risk for,
what values to have.

But the women's movement for white equality can't lift
a finger to stop male violence, because it wants to join the patriarchy as junior partners, not abolish it. There is no way to
have "career advancement" while risking your life to end oppression. And while white women don't want to feel responsible for Black Genocide, neither do they want to miss out on
the profits from it. While these white women have borrowed
powerful words and phrases from the Black struggle – "liberation", "sisters" – they don't live those ideas.

Most white women, although uneasy and worried
about the violence, have clearly decided to live with it in

order to go along with the system. Each is hoping it'll be that other woman who gets trapped by that sick guy (you know, "Otherwoman"). Their role models tell them to keep thinking about money, about how they're getting accepted by the system.

LIKE WHITE WOMEN IN NAZI GERMANY & SOUTH AFRICA

We gotta think about choices. All the time the sand is shifting underneath us. See, being white in amerikkka is like being on an escalator, carrying us upward into the structure of genocide. Everyone says that they've just picked this one little stair to perch on – "I'm not hurting anyone." But it isn't a stair, it's an escalator, and we can only not go up if we make a choice to get off.

We have to make that choice – or passively accept the choice prepared for us to be part of that genocide. Like white women in Nazi Germany and South Africa. Whether we admit it or not, each of us must make the choice of who we are. We choose to take part in genocide or to oppose it, to work for the patriarchy or to fight it with our lives. **Who we are is our choice.**

There are white women, hurt and angry, who believed that the '70s women's movement meant sisterhood, and who feel betrayed by escalator women. By women who went back home to the patriarchy. But the women's movement never left father Dick's side. You can tell that by the fact that no women died in the struggle. The jails were not filled by prisoners of that class war. There was no war. And there was no liberation. We got a share of genocide profits and we love it. We are Sisters of Patriarchy, and true supporters of oppression. We are not Black women's sisters, or Salvadorian women's sisters, not anybody's sisters except father Dick.

Patriarchy in its highest form is Euro-imperialism on a world scale. If we're Dick's sister and want what he has gotten, then in the end we support that system that he got it all from. And our own subjugation, too. Be it ever so blood soaked there's no place like home.

BOTTOMFISH BLUES

INTEGRATION
"Learn A Way To Say Goodbye"

AS THE GENOCIDE CRISIS GROWS OUT of control in amerikkka, scattering bodies everywhere, it's time to draw the balance sheet on integration and what it's really meant in the women's community. In this incredibly racist society, the women's community is almost unique in being a community that was founded with a commitment to integration. A community whose sisters think of themselves as being against racism. A community not directly controlled by white men. There is public silence among us—yet and again, the violent racial crisis shaking amerikkka is also a crisis in the women's community. But we don't wanna really look too hard at integration and what it's meant to us, to our community. This is what I mean to talk about, directly and bluntly as I can.

Let's deal with what integration really is in amerikkka. Let's strip it down. 'Cause integration has nothing to do with propaganda about black 'n white walking hand in hand into the sunset. It presupposes that there are women of at least two separate nations, one oppressor and one oppressed (else why would we need to fight to integrate?). After all, white women are in the patriarchal white amerikkkan nation. We sure don't got one of our own. We want and accept citizenship, don't we, with all its privileges and duties, in Dick's white nation? Black women aren't citizens in the white patriarchal nation. New Afrikan women are captives in amerikkka, not citizens. Integration recapitulates the old mistress-slave relationship of european to Afrikan – which is why we're not talking about integrating Indian women or Cambodian women. Just as slavery was a property relation, and segregation a property relation, so is integration a property relation at a higher historical point.

Integration presupposes something – *dis*integration. That's the hidden thing no one's talking about. If you're integrating two things then at least one thing has to go, has got to give way and disintegrate, the captured into the captors. So integration means someone's got to move, practically speaking. That's pretty clear. It's also clear that white women mean for New Afrikan women to do the moving. We sure aren't moving to leave our nation. No, they gotta leave their people and come better themselves by moving to us. Gotta leave their oppressed nation (disintegrate) and help strengthen our white nation (integrate). That's what the racial crisis is now.

Stripped of the false sentiment and the dicky propaganda, integration is a solution for political white women and a problem for New Afrikan women. No matter how loudly we deny it, we should know in our bones that what we say is sisterhood ain't nothing of the kind. Integration is an attack on New Afrikan sisterhood.

Let's check integration now, after 20 years of progress. In both spheres, both in the outside society and in the women's community. As a baseline definition, let me say that integration for us is the system that lets white women take what they need from Black women while helping them to die as a people. And the real question is, how can we as amazons get out of the genocide game?

There were two incidents about integration last year that we need to break down, really learn from. One was the case of the seven New Afrikan women-children who attacked white women on Manhattan's integrated Upper West Side. The other is the response to the Dianne Davidson controversy at last year's integrated Michigan Womyn's Music Festival. Both events became big problems for the white women concerned. Now the seven women-children are dismissed as messed-up poor kids whose mothers are fuckups, seen em one you seen em all. Who acted up and who will soon be on dope, on welfare, or in prison anyway.

i think the case of the pinpricks sez it all about integration. Last November seven New Afrikan women-children, ages 12 to 15, were arrested for hit and run attacks using pins on at least 45 women, all of whom were white except for two Asians. For those few weeks there was mass panic on the Upper West Side, calls by white women for more police protection, and stationing of extra police on each block in the area. Once they were arrested, though, white sisters breathed a sigh of relief and forgot about them. And why

Lost Souls in

Needles in Angry Ha

Why 9 neglected girls terrorized the Upper W.

By Nina Bernstein

FOR A WEEK :his :ail a hand

not? Is it really news to white women that even the children of our colony hate us?

"It isn't some mystery. It doesn't need a commission or a study," said Rakayyah Howell, who directs a local anti-truancy program. *"The root of it is real simple. It's payback."* PAYBACK, now there's an interesting idea on the horizon. In family court the woman judge, Leah Ruth Marks, delivered a racist diatribe to the girls before she found them guilty:

> *Even in this courtroom many of you reacted with joy to your victims' descriptions of the pain and fear you drove into them as you stabbed them with your weapons... it seems to me that you took joy most of the time in harming women who appeared somewhat affluent, who took pride in their personal appearance, who seemed somewhat dignified and to have some purpose in life. If that woman also had long hair and was alone, your temptation to hurt her and ability to take joy in hurting her was irresistible.*

Machine

ew York Newsday

'he children city agency 1akes nomads

Nina Bernstein

welve year-old Tonisha stands on a h-strewn sidewalk, her eyes shut tight inst the gritty wind and her own tears
    we has had no bed to call her
    she will have no bed at all
    is a toddler sexually molested
    belongs to no one but the City
    — and the city's Child Welfare
    n has made her part of its tribe
    lren
    iundreds of them, foster chil
       nightly from one temporary
    mother in a forced march that
    hronically short of sleep, food
    care, waiting for permanent
    at may never come
    is not a secret. In September
    trict Judge Mary Johnson Lowe
    brought by the Legal Aid Soci-
       then makeshift structure of

WEST SIDE ATTACKS

10 Arrests In Pin

This was after the courtroom had heard how the children were the truest victims. The oldest, a 15-year old charged as the "ringleader" (every slave rebellion must have a "ringleader" in Master's eyes), grew up in the Holland, notorious as one of NY's most violent welfare hotels. Two of the women-children, sisters age 12 and 13, eat and sleep on a bare floor in part of their grandmother's crowded apartment. The 13-year old had become the "mother" at age 7, cooking and caring for her four younger siblings. When cops broke into another place to arrest yet another of the children, they found her living involuntarily in a crack den:

"The children were all alone in the dark, shaking," recalled the woman who accompanied the police into the apartment last year. *"The four-year old was trying to cook grits on a hot plate."*

Many of their parents were already dead, usually murdered, or in prison. These women-children, *who have never known any other life than our present 20-year reign of equal rights and integration,* are fighting best they can. i for one admire their courage.

The meaning in Judge Marks' verbal abuse went beyond her casual racist assumptions: i.e. that "pride in personal appearance," "dignified," "somewhat affluent," and having "purpose in life" = WHITE. As she admits, the seven women-children didn't attack old bag ladies or poor Latinas or blue collar white women – all of whom are on the street in the highly integrated Upper West Side.

Their targets were those affluent white women of the affirmative-action generation. Precisely those upwardly-mobile professional and business white women who profited most from the struggles of the civil rights movement and the feminist movement. Who used those struggles to jump high up in Dick's empire. And what freaks those women out is precisely that their Upper West Side is so integrated. Because that's where college educated young whites have integrated housing by driving Blacks and Puerto Ricans out of block after block, building after building. Integration is a one-way street, where Third World communities disintegrate and are absorbed piecemeal into the White Planet. It wasn't the white patriarchy which these white sisters helped disintegrate, was it now?

The whole conflict was about nothing but integration, and even the kids are saying what time it is.

So after 20 years of integration, here's what it comes down to: white women talk all this "sister" shit when they want "minority" preference in jobs, but have the cops out in force to protect them from even the women-children of New Afrika. These children were sentenced at birth to terrorism, to chaos, and to early death, because our white empire no longer needs them alive and we're having a closeout sale on our ex-slave colony. We hate and fear them, we've cleverly imported millions of Latinas and Asian women to replace their labor so we don't have to do it, and now we want them to scatter and gradually die out just as the women of many Indian nations before them.

For these women-children just being alive is the real crime, and we've found them guilty as charged. Why shouldn't they strike out at the people whose everything comes from their nothing? *"It was only a natural thing that happened,"* said one 13-year old of jabbing a white woman in the face. A 13-year old girl. What's being born? Do you dare to name it? That's one reason we want a few Black women around us, to deflect the anger and to protect us from other Black Women and children.

Let's bring this closer to home. How come nobody speaks on those New Afrikan women-child amazons? Why the silence? i mean, this trial should have been an exciting event for political women. Shoulda drew women activists to it. All those women agree how brave the young women-children of Soweto are, confronting the oppressors. And the Palestinian women-children of the Intifada, hurling stones at the white oppressors. Forcing a reluctant world to bow in recognition. But when these New Afrikan women-children do the same thing right here, everyone falls silent. Are your chickens coming home to roost?

Instead, we left it to the men's press to brand them as social basket cases and their mothers as worse. So those women we destroy we forget as losers and those women who fight back we try to dismiss as losers. And we only want our white State to make it all go away (tho it won't!).

Interesting isn't it that when something "unspeakable" happens like the Central Park Rape everyone speaks on it. Everyone wants to feel involved, money and concern pour in, debate happens, there's even a defense campaign. But this which should be spoken on draws only silence. Especially, most especially, from our integrated women's community, our publications and organizations. *Womanews*, NYC's women's newspaper, belatedly had a short story on it. Neither they nor anyone else organized any support about this.

So why can't sisters who tell us all about Palestine and South Africa see the same thing when it happens right here? It has a lot to do with this phony integration, with this shining lie that we're a movement of and for *all* sisters. It's only when you admit that New Afrikans are a colonized nation, that you can see what these kids are doing – albeit crude and not thought out – as resistance against oppression.

The whole mindset of the integrated women's movement, that we are for all sisters together, shields white women from being recognized as oppressors of other women. It takes a shining vision of the future and says that's what relationships are now, instead of the harder reality we start from. Simple black and white information isn't recognized by the mind in a clean, crisp way. So the integrated women's community can't talk about the seven because to talk of the justice of women-children as incipient New Afrikan amazons would break the illusion. And you're married to the illusion.

Understand that overcoming this integration is no side issue. It's the most important thing we can do. Our shallow ideas of sisterhood and our willing complicity in men's crimes are all knotted together in our white racism, much more than we understand right now. This is the **central struggle** in our community. In the long run it will answer our first question: who the "we" are.

Last summer our racism bolted right out of the closet into the middle of the Michigan Womyn's Music Festival. There was already controversy about singer Dianne Davidson. In the Spring, an interview with the women's journal *Sojourner* had led to criticism and an intense exchange of letters. The controversy and letters in lesbian journals still continue.

Davidson comes from a small-town Southern background. From the time she was five days old she was cared for and essentially raised by her family's New Afrikan servant, Hattie Ruth Simon. Davidson sings a song sentimentalizing this relationship, in a tradition indulged in by white Southerners ever since slavery days. She also says that she "wasn't white" in her previous life and that her servant woman was sent to her by some goddess or spirits to help her make this racial transition. Or something like that.

On Friday nite when Davidson did these same things from the stage at Michigan, there was some shock and some anger. Led by New Afrikan and Latina sisters, most of them long-time Festival workers and performers, backstage discussions began about interrupting the racism.

An official Festival workers' statement was read onstage on Sunday that criticized Davidson for *"perpetuating racism,"* and ended:

> *White women must accept the responsibility to recognize and interrupt such racism in our home communities and at our community gatherings.*

On Saturday, the Festival had scheduled not merely a workshop, as is customary, but for the first time an all-festival Town Meeting on fighting racism, which 500 women took part in. One good result of that meeting was CLEAR–Chicago Lesbians Emerging Against Racism. According to a friendly article by Ginny Berson and Achy Obejas in *Windy City Times*, CLEAR began when seven white sisters who'd been thru Michigan heard that Davidson was going to perform at Mountain Moving Coffeehouse on October 28, 1989. This white group took the responsibility for interrupting our community's racism, calling a boycott of the concert and an anti-racist workshop there afterwards.

This boycott and the heated political discussions that took place around it both with Mountain Moving and in the press led to some real understanding amongst all the sisters involved. Things didn't end with the usual dismissive mea culpa.

The idea of white women acting for ourselves, in our own name, not hiding behind Third World women and men as we usually do on this subject, is so positive because it gives us another choice to what has become the dishonest soap opera of integration among us. It helped some white sisters take responsibility that is really ours, while letting Third World sisters be free to take part and relate in the ways and degrees that fit their own agenda. That really came out in the *Windy City Times* story:

"Traditionally, it's always put to women of color to explain racism," said Burgin. *"We decided that had to change."*

"Most of the sisters I know don't even know she's on the planet," said Donna Weems, president of the Literary Exchange and an activist in the Black lesbian community, by way of explaining why there's been no clamor about Davidson among Black lesbians. *"But this business of white women taking the initiative on anti-racist work is long overdue. I was heartened to hear this."*

"I think it's very good when white women try to raise their own consciousness about racism," said Carmen Aguilar, a member of Latina Lesbians En Nuestro Ambiente (LLENA). *"Of course, we too need to help frame certain issues so that they have an understanding. Besides, it's important we all be involved in order to have a real sense of community."*

To me the focus isn't Davidson. And it's wrong to make her out to be some one woman epidemic of racism. It ain't about her. It's about what the response to her in our community reveals. All along, most women in the community have considered these attitudes to be acceptable. That's the main thing. Even after her racism was out of the closet in the *Sojourner* interview and the controversy was on, the Michigan Womyn's Music Festival still thought it ok for her to perform. No problem. And even after the protest from Festival workers and her refusal to admit anything wrong – feminist coffeehouses and concert-goers still thought her ok. No problem.

It's only 'cause the women she steps on are New Afrikan that we think it's ok. If a visiting white South African singer had popped up at Michigan to say how nice it was that her Afrikan servant from Soweto loved her, and if one Afrikan sister in the audience had protested, Ms. Boer would have been sent flying. Instant apologies all around. But New Afrikan women, ah, that's different to us somehow. That's what the Davidson controversy revealed.

The ugliest thing at Michigan by far was the booing that greeted the Festival Workers Statement (mixed in with cheers and applause). It was good that so many sisters came to the Town Meeting about fighting racism, but the

vast majority chose not to take part. **Aren't we reaching a
nodal point, where even the routine pretense of sisterhood
is coming apart? Among us as in the larger society. When
we don't care to fake it anymore?** Lots of us were shocked
that sisters would boo an anti-racist statement, or that Alix
Dobkin (who read it and is one of the most respected white
musicians in the women's community) would be booed by
women. But i think it was good, it got folks' real loyalties
out there. It was an honest expression of integration among
white lesbians and feminists.

FACT: Hundreds of white women were pissed that
Third World and white sisters angry about racism against
New Afrikan women were taking up time in our once a year
lesbian vacation, when we wanna celebrate the sheer freedom of living in a women-only environment. There's an attitude that "their" job is to entertain us, but otherwise we want
"them" outnumbered so it's all ours. Our racism is edging
more and more out there, as Dick's genocide gains momen-
tum and all white folks get more cocky. Many white sisters
feel they don't even have to pretend to care anymore.

What i'm saying is that it's not Dianne Davidson who's
the outsider. That her view, her integration with her very own
New Afrikan woman, is representative of something very
deep in our community and in our "women's culture." Sure,
Dianne Davidson loves her New Afrikan servant woman – why
shouldn't she? Her "mammy" cooked her food and washed
up after her, cleaned her clothes, took care of her, taught her
and kept her company. One way all the way. Why shouldn't
she love that? That's why lots of white Southern *men*, from
Robert E. Lee to Buford Bigot, have always went on how they
love their "mammy." And they all say they're not racists, too.
Dianne Davidson boasts how she's a daring non-conformist,
a "rule-breaker" as she puts it. White women have bought
into this image because it flatters themselves, but Davidson's
beliefs are as "nonconformist" as the confederate flag.

New Afrikan sisters have been pointing out this "black mammy" shit to white feminists for oh, about 150 years or so now. Maybe we should have a centennial celebration, at least. Every year they have to start all over, repeat it again. Somehow, someway, white women with college degrees and phd's, who run olivia records, can't remember this basic thing. *Now,* in 1990 (after over 20 years of integration) it's still a *controversy* to us—maybe "Black mammies" are good, maybe it's bad, we don't know. 'Course, what it is, is we don't care. Dianne Davidson isn't anything special—she's our cultural representative. Because in our culture, New Afrikan women are an appliance to us, our feminist property to improve our lives, to entertain us and support our community, to make it even easier to be white. Hey, what happens to them and their real children we don't care—they can go die unless we need them for some reason.

It's kinda dialectical. i mean, who needs to integrate? White sisters like to say, we love to say, we have so much to offer (politics, resources) while Black women have so little. Without our help they're powerless. But, lady, white women ain't got nothing yet of our own to give. Nothing but money. Nothing but some thing we're dependent on white men's power for. Better believe it.

It isn't Black women who need white women's resources, it's white women who need Black women's resources. That's why, without ever posing it as a conscious decision, white women have almost universally chosen not to form white women's groups to fight racism in our community, but took up urging integration on Black women as a substitute.

Twenty years ago at the start of the modern women's movement, this situation existed: There was a struggle for Black Power and independence. There was a struggle for Sisterhood, with sisterhood being defined as all women. Our politics were taken mostly from the Black movement, at least many key ideas—separatism, consciousness-raising, and identification with the oppressed on a world scale. Although the situation in the Black movement was very reactionary in terms of women, there was a general symmetry between political Black men and political white women that New Afrikan women should be integrated into both of these movements. **And throughout the 20 years, New Afrikan women have remained marginalized inside both movements that claim them as property (it's your typical joint custody fight).**

New Afrikan women have strongly resisted inside both movements. Many refuse to deal much with either movement and
are searching for better answers.

White women needed New Afrikan women in a big way.
Need to steal their politics and culture, need them as front
women, need to colorize the white women's movement. Need
to disguise the lack of serious politics among white women.
The situation is the same today.

It's white women, as the largest and best-educated and
best-connected "minority" in the affirmative-action scam,
that have profited most in new careers, promotions, business
ventures, property ownership, and upward stepping mobility.
Dick grumbles at having to share anything from his plate,
but he needs us to help him keep the loot within the Great
White Family. It would be hard to get away with our white
power feminism if everyone saw it as it is, so we need to colorize our community a little. We need just enough Women
of Color–but never so many that our agenda would be
changed... So we can pretend we're for *all* women, not just
ms. number one.

Which is why we need to steal New Afrikan women's
politics. So we can claim to have a women's consciousness that
we don't have. You have only to look at the Dianne Davidson
mess–or a thousand others–to figure out that we, just by
ourselves, aren't anti-racist at all. We can repeat the words
by rote but we don't know how to live it. Left to our lone-
some we'd look like politically backward, insensitive white
bigots. That's why we need them as our cleaning women, to
keep washing up our community, keep wiping the dirt off
our faces. Fronting for us. We leave it to Third World women
to catch the worst racist "slips," to protest. Then we say, "Our
community is fighting racism." No, ain't no "our," no "we."
They are doing it and we're coasting off it. And, of course, we
need their energy and strength and ideas to help build Jane's
house. To help build institutions and organizations that are

our property and that they get something out of (else they wouldn't do it), but which will never be theirs.

Black women are unique to us. We got a special thing about them, which you and i know in our guts but we can't talk about in public. Unlike Indian or German or Palestinian women, we deny New Afrikan women their nationality. Alone, of all the women on the face of the earth. No one denies that Lakota women or Nicaraguan women have their own nation whose situation and struggles they are part of. But Black sisters, we really feel that they are ours, out of hundreds of years of their involuntary sharing and involuntary caring for us. We demand that they stay by our side, be a "gift" to our community to help us make this transition. To give it their strength and their soul. It's more important that New Afrikan women educate us and help us than take care of their own–our problems come first. We demand that they leave their nation for us.

'Course we put it on New Afrikan women's weakness. Say Black men are too violent, too homophobic, too islamic, too everything for them to deal with. Think we're doing the charitable thing, always skimming some of the most conscious New Afrikan women for our community. Take the few and leave the many. Do we really believe that New Afrikan sisters can't take care of themselves? i don't know what direction New Afrikan women will choose. How they will solve their problems. But i do know they ain't on earth to solve mine.

The thing is, we really fear New Afrikan women even more than we do men. When the Black pin-prick hysteria on the Upper West Side was going on, I couldn't help thinking of *The Birds*. You know, that old Alfred Hitchcock movie. Here we just assume those birds are out there, flying 'round doing their harmless thing, for us to use however we feel like. Shoot em out of the sky for fun, listen to their music for lifting our souls, then roast em up for din-din. Love those birds.

But *then* ("It's not nice to fool Mother Nature!") the birds get the word and everywhere around the world, white civilization perishes as billions of fed-up birds, in relentless waves, swarm over and peck to death every last white person. Wow! Movie-goers were terrified. Whites were shocked that they'd never thought of the obvious—you mean something we use and take for granted might resent us, might do *payback?* i think it wasn't birds that whites were so unconsciously guilty and worried about. We know that what we've done to New Afrikan women for generation after generation is so cruel and anti-woman that if it were us and if we got the chance for payback—why we'd...

That's why the panic last Fall, when white women were taking cabs to their front doors after work, only going out with escorts, avoiding Black women, wanting more police protection... All 'cause of seven women-children.

When i speak on the silence in our community about all this, i'm not talking about evil people—i wanna emphasize that—but about the degrading and anti-woman effects on all of us from this phony integration. Sisters work for years at educating and building, only to see things slide backwards time after time. Look at *Womanews*, which has always been one of the most serious local women's newspapers. A real survivor from the 1970s.

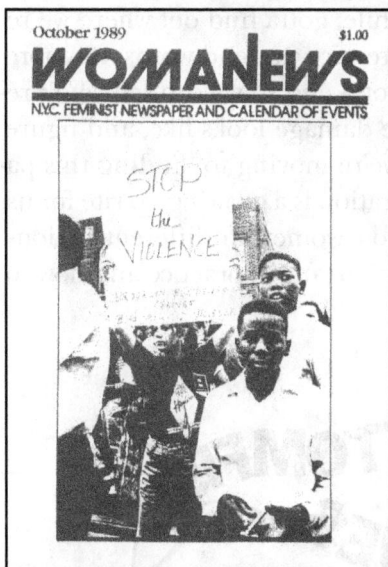

October 1989 $1.00

WOMANEWS

N.Y.C. FEMINIST NEWSPAPER AND CALENDAR OF EVENTS

STOP the VIOLENCE

Like most women's projects, it was integrated in the usual sense—mostly white sisters with a few die-hard women of color. That gradually changed as more women of color came around and they began demanding more respect. Finally, Third World sisters' complaints about continued racism led them to forming a caucus, taking the steering wheel and demanding that white sisters get themselves together. Overnight, white women fled. According to an account in their pages a few months ago, there is now only one white sister left full-time on *Womanews*. So years and years of integration has added up to feminist "white flight." And a telling situation where women of color put out a newspaper whose primary beneficiaries and readers are white women, while there is yet no New Afrikan or Latina women's newspaper in NYC. Just like every conference ends with angry words and Third World women's caucuses and complaints of racism.

Some sisters worry that moving to upfront white groups and bringing up racism will be a dangerous mess (that fear should fax something to us FAST), that then the racism will get really ugly. Yup, that's what i'd guess too. But let it all out. The storm is coming to amerikkka anyway. White sisters gotta stand alone for awhile, gotta find out where we really are. No cover-up, no more nice pretend words, no more using Women of Color. It's gotta end so we can tell who's really into sisterhood, what the damage looks like, and figure out based on reality where we're moving to. Ending this patriarchal soap opera of integration is a growing up rite for us. Only then can we explore how women in different nations can be united. Explore what it means in practice and how to relate as equals.

IF IT WERE EASY, MEN WOULD DO IT TOO.

sarah jessica parker

I DON'T KNOW HOW SHE DOES IT

U.S.Military SEXUAL TERROR

MISSING

"None are more hopelessly enslaved than those who falsely believe they are free." -Goethe

Eyes: Brown

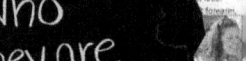

DIERS RAPED BY ARMY
GHT WAR ON TWO FRONTS

DAILY NEWS
NEW YORK'S HOMETOWN NEWSPAPER
.I. murder suspect tells co

I KILLED
7 WOMEN

STILL NO ANSWERS

oledo truck driver De mus Colvin's recent confession c seve der cases of pros

Text visible within the illustration:

WE INTEND TO BEAT THE NEGRO IN THE BATTLE OF LIFE, AND DEFEAT MEANS ONE THING — EXTERMINATION — BIRMINGHAM ALA. NEWS.

KKK

NO COMPROMISE. NO UNIFICATION. BUT A WHITEMAN'S GOVERNMENT OR RUIN AND EXTERMINATION

CALL HOME YOUR TROOPS

OFFICE OF U.S. MARSHAL.

NEGRO POPULATION ... THING OUT ... VE PLACE, TO ... TE MEN.

As an appendix, we have added a related but very different kind of article: "The Ideas of Black Genocide in the Amerikkkan Mind." It was written in 2009 by Butch Lee and J. Sakai, and was first passed around (although not published) as part of a collection of post-"Katrina" working papers on the New Afrikan crisis within the u.s. empire. We are using it because it gives readers some larger background of how Black Genocide has always been present and publicly discussed throughout the u.s. empire's life. It is about how the "new normal" of euro-capitalism is always being violently engineered in blueprints of blood and cash.

THE IDEAS of Black Genocide in the Amerikkkan Mind

IT IS TRUE THAT NO NATION in the world was more purely formed out of genocide than the u.s. empire. What Adolf Hitler only wanted to be, what the Nazi movement aspired to be, amerikkka already was. It is laughable to think of amerikkka as a "post-racial" society, but it certainly is a "post-holocaust" one. It is inescapable, then, that many thoughts about genocide, the ideas and theories of genocide, have likewise always been present within amerikkkan society.

Any major change in society is always surrounded by a cloud of ideas, like energy particles, preceding the change. Preparing people for it. While also unifying and guiding and correcting society's mass activity so that the social machinery stays on course. Ideas that are active factors but often concealed under other names, wearing other guises. **Which is why studying the *ideas and theories* of genocide as they have existed here is so important right now.**

For example: Too often, those of us who fight for justice can feel the reality of genocide, but cannot grab hold of it in a practical sense. It somehow evades us and slides out of our grasp. Because we have been conditioned *not* to see that genocide is rooted in gender. That it works through gender-class no less than race or nation. This is beyond what we will fully get into here, but we wanted to point out the future of this discussion.

The understandings of Black Genocide have evolved on *both* sides. Two sides have been struggling to control people's thinking about Black Genocide for generations now, and this is what our story is about–those ideas. What were crude visions of bloodthirsty battles and mass burials became more imaginative, even fantasy-like in some cases, until they matured into our present. When the horrors of the earliest settler his-story are being repeated now, but on a higher level in an opposite, more sophisticated form. Always around the hidden fulcrum of gender-class, around which everything human revolves. This is complex and well-disguised for an operation so vast, but we will open it up.

The violent reshaping of New Orleans after the catastrophic flooding of "Hurricane Katrina" in 2005, raised the question of New Afrikan genocide. Particularly after even politicians admitted that the disaster was one of winning or losing race politics. *"New Orleans is not going to be as black as it was for a long time, if ever again,"* confidently declared u.s. secretary of housing & urban development Alphonso Jackson.

While Louisiana settler congressman Richard Baker said it was a victory to get rid of poor New Afrikans: *"We finally cleaned up public housing in New Orleans. We couldn't do it, but God did."*

But what seemed starkly simple right after Katrina, is more complex than it appears. Especially for the role of New Afrikan women. Even in the Congressional hearings after Katrina in 2005, they couldn't "white out" the inevitable question of genocide. As NBC News reported: *"Black survivors of Hurricane Katrina said Tuesday that racism contributed to the slow disaster response, at times likening themselves in emotional congressional testimony to victims of genocide and the Holocaust."*

Rep. Jeff Miller, Republican from Florida, used his microphone to try and override the New Afrikan women survivors, saying that "genocide" as a description wasn't accurate. Since, as the white Republican politician put it: "not a single person was marched into a gas chamber and killed." But community activist Leah Hodges answered sharply: *"We left body bags behind... The people of New Orleans were stranded in a flood and were allowed to die."* During the hearings, called for by former Congresswoman Cynthia McKinney, *"another woman said military troops focused machine gun laser targets on her granddaughter's forehead. Others said their families were called racial epithets by police."*

While the possibility of Black Genocide may now seem nearly overhead, it really has been difficult to fully understand. Right now, years after the partial ethnic cleansing of New Orleans, the word "genocide" is still being dramatically thrown down but almost never used in strategy or critical analysis. Most don't even know that several generations ago there was a major New Afrikan community debate coast-to-coast about the imminent possibility of genocide. Or how that debate ended. And no one is linking today's New Afrikan crisis to the unanswered alert called in by a radical woman a generation ago.

THE IDEA OF THE NECESSITY
OF "EXTERMINATION"

For many years, the "great" plantation-capitalist and u.s. president Thomas Jefferson has been an unexpected headliner in our cultural news. Dramatic articles popping up unexpectedly in our daily press, best-selling books, getting spotlighted on television network national news. Everything but "Entertainment Tonight" and YouTube. All focused on the keyhole into his sex life, what do you expect? This being a completely capitalist culture. So now it's accepted as fact, that the long ago prez, the much-honored "Sage of Monticello," kept Sally Hemings as his sex slave for many years until his death. That wasn't surprising to anyone.*

    Jefferson, one of the Virginia "great planter" ruling class, is usually considered the most intellectual and philosophical of u.s. leaders. What is definitely not getting discussed on prime time is that he was an early leader in promoting the idea of Black Genocide. Jefferson argued that this was something which should be justified by euro-settler society as *self-defense*. This set an important precedent, and from Thomas Jefferson all the way to George Zimmerman

---

* Sally Hemings was a famous captive New Afrikan domestic worker on the plantation of former u.s. president Thomas Jefferson. The subject of tabloid scandals even in Jefferson's lifetime, Hemings is now the center of best-selling books, DNA investigations and historians' conferences. She was born before the u.s.a. was formed, and died in 1835 still a captive. What was striking is that though held in chattel slavery, she was the biological half-sister of Jefferson's wife, Martha Wayles Jefferson. The half-sisters greatly resembled each other. After Martha Wayles's death, Jefferson secretly used Sally Hemings as a replacement. Her six subsequent children were fathered by Jefferson, who freed the surviving Heming children when grown unlike any other New Afrikan children he had held captive for his plantation business.

the American "tradition" is that killing any or all New Afrikans is always excusable as *self-defense.*

Back then they didn't say "genocide," of course, since this is a modern 20th century term. Back then they usually said "extermination," a blunt term which implies a cleansing away of the inferior in the interests of the superior. As in, "exterminating pests and diseases."

The heart of the issue back then to our prison-warden president was the growing reality of widespread violent New Afrikan slave rebellions. Which in a white nightmare could end up in the millions of the formerly en-slaved hunting down the white population.

Jefferson believed this to be quite possible. Since even if voluntarily emancipated by law or charity, the poor and bitter ex-slaves would still harbor murderous thoughts and plots for revenge. *"We have the wolf by the ears, and can neither hold him, nor safely let him go. Justice is on one scale, and self-preservation in the other."* Jefferson argued that the violent kid-napping, transport, mass torture, murdering, and en-slaved labor of millions for generations must *"divide us into parties, and produce convulsions which will probably never end but in the* **extermination** *of the one or the other race."* (our emphasis)

This was a popular opinion in the founding years of the "American Republic." After his travels in the new u.s. empire, which resulted in his famous classic, *Democracy in America,* the French aristocrat Alexis de Tocqueville wrote that any unchaining of the New Afrikans would tragically result in *"the most horrible of civil wars"* and *"perhaps in the* **extermination** *of one or the other of the two races."* Because he believed that the Europeans as the superior race – i.e., as the human bearers of euro-capitalism – will by their very nature wipe out all those they cannot usefully enslave: *"The European is to the other races of mankind what mankind himself is to the lower animals: he makes them subservient to his use, and when he cannot subdue he* **destroys** *them."*

Even the frontier novelist, James Fenimore Cooper (author of *Last of the Mohicans, Leatherstockings,* and other classic u.s. novels), argued that: *"The time must come when American Slavery must cease... The struggle that will follow, will necessarily be a war of **extermination**."* Over and over again, back then, the word "extermination" comes up in the euro-settler mind. (our emphasis all cases above)

That famous novelist's sentiments only demonstrate how matter of fact whites were in general about *genocide,* whether against Indians or New Afrikans or anybody else. General Sam Houston of Texas even argued that since euro-settlers had often wiped out Indians and taken their lands – and since euro-settlers felt that Mexicans were no better than Indians – then the u.s. empire should replace the entire Mexican nation, too. "I see no reason why we should not go on the same course, now, and take their land."

As anyone knows from the slightest knowledge of u.s. his-story and the old Hollywood "Westerns," exterminating troublesome colonized nations and peoples is part of the euro-settler empire's masculine national culture. And proud of it, too. Even in the 20th century these views were visibly dominant, majority views. For example: President Theodore Roosevelt, who helped found the u.s. national park system and tried to be an example of the macho outdoors man, could casually write off indigenous nations and peoples as among the pests that had to be exterminated (although he briefly tried to pose as a "friend" to New Afrikans). To that u.s. president, the true manhood of the master race was only refreshed by tapping the spirit of mass murders.

> *I suppose I should be ashamed to say that I take the Western view of the Indian. I don't go so far as to think that the only good Indians are the dead Indians, but I believe nine out of ten are, and I shouldn't inquire too closely into the case of the tenth. The most vicious cowboy has more moral principle than the average Indian.*

Remember, that was the president of the united states talking. Having ideas about the necessity of genocide, and discussing those ideas pro or con, were casual matters to euro-capitalist society back then. So common that they were what was defined as "normal." Just another day at the office. Everyone knew people who were taking part in these questions. If not someone in the family, then neighbors or businessmen you dealt with or politicians you listened to at election rallies. It was no big deal. Except that it was.

INCREASINGLY VIOLENT CRISIS AND IMAGINARY SOLUTIONS

The question of doing genocide to New Afrikans suddenly became much more intense during prison-warden and u.s. president George Washington's term in office, when the Haitian slave revolution of 1791 could not be put down. Even with Napoleon's army, as well as the invading regiments of British and Spanish troops. The people's war against euro-capitalist colonial slavery in Haiti raged for thirteen years, and ended in the complete elimination of the euro-settler population on the island. At the very end, euro-settlers were being executed to the last person, children and women included. It was estimated that some 100,000 Europeans, including soldiers, and 60,000 Afrikans had lost their lives in the many years of fighting over the French colony, which the French empire had named "St. Domingue." It was renamed "Haiti" by the victorious rebels, restoring the indigenous name for the territory.

Few foreign events have had more effect on the u.s. empire than the Haitian Revolution of 1791–1804, and our two nations have been intimately linked ever since then.

**Although, as usual, most euro-settlers today are totally
clueless to all that.**

The 1791 Haitian Revolution was the very first successful working-class revolution in the New World, and it was
done by en-slaved Afrikans. It called like a bell to Afrikans
throughout the hemisphere, and caused the start of the u.s.
tradition of phoney "humanitarian aid" in foreign countries.
What has from the start been a completely dishonest and
perverse policy of "aid" to help repressing the oppressed.
Which is why it is so sharply fitting that the u.s. empire is the
chief overseer of the multi-billion dollar charitable "aid" al-
legedly for the countless victims of the massive January 2010
earthquake in Haiti, which electrified the world. Never before has an unnatural disaster come so close to wiping out
an entire country. And the u.s. empire like a great leech is
hanging in there, stopping as much help as possible from
reaching the dispossessed, trying to have as many Haitians
die and be tortured as possible.

So back in 1791, it is no surprise that u.s. settlers here
were horrified that Afrikan slaves in Haiti had freed themselves and were rebelling against their European colonial-
ists. Immediate u.s. "aid" to help the French settlers there
kill and re-enslave Afrikan workers was promised by prison-
warden & u.s. president George Washington. Prison-warden
Thomas Jefferson, then the u.s. secretary of state, ordered
"one thousand stand of arms and other military stores" and $40,000
cash sent right away. That was just the beginning of a large
u.s. relief effort for the European jailors on the rebellion-
torn island, which went on for years. Giving in to French re-
quests that old loans owed to the fallen French monarchy be
instead immediately repaid to the embattled French plant-
ers in Haiti, the u.s. sent another $400,000 (a large sum of
money in those days).

And year after year, the u.s. treasury guaranteed
St. Domingue's flimsy promissory notes ordering desperately

The 2010 Earthquake

In the 7.2 Richter reading quake on January 12, 2010, much of even official Haiti seemed to disappear. The Presidential Palace, the National Assembly building, the chief Catholic Holy Trinity cathedral, the capital's main prison and art museums alike, the large UN Mission headquarters, and many other important structures collapsed into dust and rubble. At the other end of the class scale, in the Haitian squatter villages typically perched on unstable hillsides and other marginal land, the catastrophe was even more severe. Communities disappeared. No actual count of the dead, wounded and displaced even exists, with death estimates wildly varying from 90,000 to 300,000.

The immediate u.s. imperial response was solely to militarily occupy Haiti to prevent any revolution from below. Before any Red Cross or other u.s. "aid" was sent, units of u.s. paratroopers landed to take over the only major airport and the capitol. In fact, for days afterwards desperately needed medical resupply airflights were waved off, denied landing permission by u.s. military air controllers who had orders to prioritize u.s. weapons supply and troop reinforcement landings.

Haiti was more devastated than if it had been A-bombed. Although billions were swiftly pledged worldwide in "aid" for Haiti, little actual "aid" has reached the people. According to 2013 International Monetary Fund research, even three years later there still are 219,000 homeless refugees making do in 352 temporary camps. There are still 2 million squatters. Adding injury to injury, last year some 7,000 Haitians died in the ongoing cholera epidemic. Which had been spread from infected UN Nepalese mercenary soldiers, brought in to protect capitalism from possible revolts. Neither the u.s. empire nor its front-man, the UN, has even pretended to be very interested in stopping the epidemic. The more inconveniently poor Haitians who die the better, from their imperial point of view. All this perverse parody of "aid" is not anything new, but what the u.s. empire's heterosexual forced marriage with Haiti has always been like.

needed food and medical supplies and arms on credit. Too bad the working-class Haitian earthquake victims of today can't get high-level u.s. government credit for everything they need, like that.

In the u.s., municipalities and church groups and individual states from New York to South Carolina also raised emergency relief funds for white refugees from Haiti. It was a popular cause among many euro-settlers. Who saw in the distressed state of the other colonialist refugees a sympathetic reflection of themselves. It is believed that approximately 25,000 French refugees found shelter in the new u.s. empire, with the greatest number resettled in Louisiana and Virginia. In 1793, for instance, French royalist general Francois Galbaud, driven from Haiti both by the Afrikan rebellion and by Frenchmen loyal to the new Jacobin revolutionary government in France, arrived in the port of Norfolk, Virginia with eight warships, escorting a civilian fleet of 137 ships full of fleeing euro-settlers. And many of their still captive Afrikan workers.

This was the political dynamite that blew up old agendas. And blew up the slave trade. It was the dangerous *"introduction of slaves into this country, or of the maroons, brigands, or cut-throats from St. Domingue,"* as Virginia u.s. congressman John Randolph warned, that suddenly woke euro-settlers up. These Haitians were former Afrikan and Indian imprisoned workers who had years of knowledge about rebellion and successfully subverting the Slave System. They had seen White Power overcome, and owned post-graduate degrees in unrest. They were the last persons in the world that euro-settlers here wanted in daily contact with their own captives. Teachers in chains. And, yet, they had been imported by the thousands, sold and scattered to countless businesses and plantations.

The influence of the Haitian revolution, through the plantation-to-plantation grapevine, became evident very quickly. Congressman Randolph in 1793 testified that he had personally overheard two New Afrikans near his house talk of killing "whites" just like *the blacks has killed the whites in the French islands and took it a little while ago.*" Other euro-settlers reported that contact with captive workers from Haiti made their own en-slaved workers "very insolent." Alarmed reports and rumors became common in the euro-settler press.

Today we have to understand this in practical military perspective. In Haiti at the time of the revolution, there were approximately 40,000 French settlers trying unsuccessfully to rule over 400,000 en-slaved Afrikan plantation laborers. Escapes were common, and in mountainous Haiti there were large, permanent Maroon colonies of rebels who were armed and developing their own guerrilla armies. So when Jefferson saw that in his Virginia, New Afrikans and settlers were roughly 50–50 population-wise, and that Maroon colonies of escaped New Afrikans persisted, the military fears did not seem unusual.

On the night of January 8, 1811, from the outer ring of plantations surrounding New Orleans, as many as five hundred Afrikan fighters came together for a bold, insurrectionary march on the city. Their plan was to seize all of lower Louisiana, and set up their own New Afrikan government. Only the intervention of federal troops aided by local settler militia overcame them. The Afrikan fighters were shockingly impressive, wearing militia uniforms and bearing muskets, both liberated from the plantations they had started by overrunning. Many of the formerly en-slaved had rudimentary experience with firearms as professional warriors back in Afrika. Others joined with axes and sugar cane cutting knives. Beating drums, they grouped themselves in eleven ethnic formations, which shared languages and fighting styles. Dread Akan warriors and other tribes from the large Asante kingdom, Kongolese, Muslim Senegambians, those from Sierra Leone, from Cuba, and so on.

Roughly equal in number to the settler troops they met in battle outside of New Orleans, the Afrikans' shortage of ammunition for their guns soon tipped the balance against them. Sixty-six were killed, with many others executed later. So stricken were the settler authorities by the gravity of their situation, that a special effort was made to terrorize those still en-slaved. Many of the slain were decapitated and their heads displayed in public places. Even in defeat, though, that rebellion smoldered and shed sparks. Hundreds of the rebels had escaped, either to small Maroon colonies in the swamps, or back to the original plantations they had left, professing that they had only been hiding in the bush and were not involved in the uprising. But they could still spread stories in the en-slaved barracks. In fact, all over the South, there was a continual stream of executions amidst charges of discovered prison plots. As late as 1822, in the failed Denmark Vesey mass conspiracy to rise up and capture Charlestown, SC, captive-labor capitalists were agitated to learn of the conspirators' letters to the Haitian government secretly seeking assistance.

This is why we need to remember the importance of having our own timeline in mind. Not the isolated, fast-food his-stories that capitalism wants us to numb our minds with. The Haitian revolution wasn't just about Haiti. Wasn't just that one island. Just as the 1960s radicalism right here was pushed and taught by *and then became part of* the anti-colonial revolutions sweeping the world. So, too, the greatest single jolt of political education that en-slaved New Afrikans in the u.s. empire ever received was from Haiti. The game-changing lesson of the Haitian revolution of 1791–1804. It wasn't an accident that the large-scale New Afrikan uprisings and mass escapes here happened *after* that political lesson was received. Part of what Black people everywhere in this Hemisphere are today, part of what "democracy" is in this continent, came from the Haitian people in their birth pains.

When we scan it on a timeline, we can immediately see all the new connections. That the Haitian revolution and the slave rebellions in the u.s. empire and the new democratic working-class revolutions leading up to 1848 in Old Europe, were parts of the *same* wave. Not isolated events belonging only to that country or this country. That all were class expressions of the contradictions within the world start-up of industrial euro-capitalist production & distribution. An interlocked, global system of industrial production & distribution initially capitalized by–and heavily dependent upon–en-slaved colonial labor, including and especially the labor of women and children. Even in the early British factories, remember, the workforce was mostly English women and children, together with emigrant colonial workers from Ireland and Scotland. All driven to the brutal, dangerous, life-stealing production line by the lash of hunger. "Free" English men didn't become "wage-slaves" at factory labor then. That all these revolutions were based in class, and were *anti-capitalism* as colonial workers had known it, is an important fact for us to know.

> *While the general usage in the u.s. empire is to use the terms "slavery" and "slave trade" to refer to Afrikan chattel slavery – and we follow this – the reader should be aware that other forms of slavery were not banned. Legal slavery of indigenous peoples continued well after the Civil War, and contrary to what everyone believes was not ended in the u.s. until 1962. State enslavement of New Afrikans has waxed and waned according to the circumstances, but remains legal to this day. And the legal enslavement of women as a gender-class continued well into the 20th century in the u.s. empire, as well as elsewhere in the modern capitalist sphere.*

The immediate result among the settlers was the movement to stop the dangerous importation of more politicized Afrikan slaves. While we are usually told that the u.s. movement to abolish the Afrikan slave trade was done for humanitarian reasons, in reality such a ban was as popular in the South as it was in the North. Fed by the hysteria in the Slave South over the revolutionary infection of Haitian and other West Indian slaves. In fact, the very first state to ban the slave trade was South Carolina, in 1792. Followed that same year by laws in Georgia and Virginia banning the importation of West Indian slaves. North Carolina and Maryland fell in line as well. In 1808, Congress banned the importation of Afrikan slaves as a whole.

Which was hailed not only by the New England abolitionists, but by some of the large slaveowners. The scarcer new captured Afrikans were on the auction block, after all, then the more the young slaves bred on their own large plantations were worth as human capital. Thomas Jefferson, for example, was unhappy that his overseers failed to understand that it wasn't the field labor but the reproduction of en-slaved women that was the ripest profit center of his entire plantation:

His interest in increasing his slave property was again revealed in a letter to his manager regarding a "breeding woman." Referring to the "loss of 5 little ones in 4 years," he complained that the overseers did not permit the slave women to devote as much time as was necessary to the care of their children. "They view their labor as the 1st object and the raising of their children but as secondary," Jefferson continued. "I consider the labor of a breeding woman as no object, and that a child raised every 2 years is of more profit than the crop of the best laboring man."

While Jefferson believed that Black Genocide was justified by u.s. "self-defense," however bloody the circumstances, he offered what he thought was an ingenious alternative. His calculations rejected the idea of simply slaughtering all the en-slaved in military campaigns (or mass New Afrikan repatriation away from the continent) as economically impractical. The prison-warden president estimated that it would cost some $600 million in lost human property to the capitalists, which was unacceptable to them. And if the New Afrikans were shipped away to Afrika after being freed, that would add another $300 million in transportation costs, by Jefferson's estimates. Together that would total about 45 times the annual export earnings of the u.s. empire's entire economy. A staggering sum, which would bankrupt euro-settler society.

His dis-utopian solution was to keep working all the adult New Afrikans until their deaths, while

prison-warden rapist
Thomas Jefferson

**removing all their infants so that as a people they would
soon cease to exist.**

> *...The only* **"practicable"** *plan, he thought, was to deport
> the future generations of blacks: Black infants would
> be taken from their mothers and trained in industri-
> ous occupations until they had reached a proper age for
> deportation. Since a newborn infant was worth only
> $25.50, Jefferson calculated, the estimated loss of slave
> property would be reduced from $600 million to only
> $37.5 million.*

> *Jefferson suggested they be transported to the independent
> black nation of Santo Domingo [Haiti].* **"Suppose the
> whole annual increase to be sixty thousand effective
> births, fifty vessels, of four hundred tons burthen each,
> constantly employed in that short run, would carry off
> the increase of every year, and the old stock would die
> off in the ordinary course of nature, lessening from its
> commencement until its final disappearance."** *He was
> confident the effects of his plan would be* **"blessed"**. *As
> for the taking of children from their mothers, Jefferson
> remarked:* **"The separation of infants from their moth-
> ers... would produce some scruples of humanity. But
> this would be straining at a gnat..."**

And "Americans" think that the Nazis were mental! Notice
that in "our" prison-warden president's "blessed" plan, New
Afrikans are referred to as "stock," as in livestock. That in
reality most of the removed infants would die, and that the
wonderful end of the plan wasn't anyone's freedom but "final
disappearance." In other words, this is just how to arrange
the capitalist economics of a more gradual and smoother
Black Genocide. If this sounds so extreme that you think it
could never have happened, remember that it bears certain
inner similarities to u.s. government programs today.

What was really utopian was believing that the plantation capitalists would ever give away their human capital, or
that the "American Republic" at that time could ever do without its second most important source of no-cost, unwaged
labor. Thomas Jefferson, despite his years of searching for
a way to commit Black Genocide, eagerly kept purchas-
ing en-slaved New Afrikans throughout his life. Even after
the passage of Virginia state law permitting the freeing of
New Afrikans by plantation owning capitalists, the wealthy
Jefferson refused to free any. Ending up his life with 267
on his plantation accounts, far more than he started with.
Nor did he free his en-slaved workers in his will, except for
the family he secretly had with Sally Hemings. Parting New
Afrikans from the planter class that rose up on their involuntary labors would be neither easy nor peaceful.

But the idea of "Colonization," of removing the New
Afrikan population by encouraging gradual mass repatriation to the West Indies or to the Liberian territory in Afrika
or to anywhere far away, nevertheless soon became popular
among euro-settlers. In 1816 the American Colonization
Society was formed, at the same time as many state colonization groups were active. Ships were chartered, New Afrikan
volunteers were recruited and outfitted with minimal supplies, and unsuccessful attempt after attempt was made to
establish ex-slave communities in other lands.

These were all-white NGOs, which had an opportunistic mix of both anti-slavery and pro-slavery supporters. One of the main ideological foundations of this strange movement was the belief that New Afrikans could not be permitted to stay in the u.s. because of the dangers of violent insurrection. As James G. Birney, the Kentucky abolitionist and presidential candidate, said: *"If the Colonization Society does not dissipate the horror of darkness which overhangs... southern society, we are undone."*

Removal through Colonization was never a real possibility. It was another dis-utopian solution, which had only a seeming rationality to it. That ignored all economics and social-political realities. As though a mix of formerly enslaved, most of whom were born in the Americas to parents savagely kidnapped long ago from the Ivory Coast and Ghana and similar places, would fit right into completely different areas of Afrika. Where they had no ties and didn't speak any of the languages and knew nothing of the local way of life and agriculture and politics. They might as well have been talking of just dumping excess New Afrikans in one-way trips to Central American jungles (a strange proposal liked by one leader named Abraham Lincoln, who even had it tried out at the cost of some New Afrikan lives).

The importance of the 19th century Colonization movement to relocate unwanted but feared captive Afrikans on other continents was not in its stated goals. Its importance was similar to that of today's Anti-Immigration movement of the "white right." As a relief valve for euro-settler distress over the barbed side-effects of antagonistic relations between oppressor and oppressed inside the empire. Because behind the Colonization movement was the idea that this entire continent was reserved for the exclusive use of the capitalist man, and that everyone else must shrink or otherwise adapt down to fit his needs – or be removed entirely. Colonization was just a different cultural metaphor for Black genocide.

THE DISAPPEARING NEGRO AND
THE WHITE MALE CONTINENT

Too often, the early bloodthirsty politics of the "American Republic" are dismissed as something irrelevant and dusty. Old bigotry, or maybe just ignorance that modern society has outgrown and left far behind us, supposedly. This has been more like a clever propaganda exercise, like replacing Bush's "evil" imperial armed occupation of Afghanistan with Obama's "friendly" imperial armed occupation of Afghanistan. What were roughly hewn, crude but basic ideas of how the social system they were building would be structured, are intensely relevant today. More than people want to admit. *"The tradition of all dead generations weighs like a nightmare on the brains of the living."*

The propaganda lie is that his-story is as one-way as time's arrow, always moving us forward away from old injustices. Reality is multilayered, dialectical and thus contradictory, and deadlier. Everything has changed, yes, and yet it is also true that what was old and overthrown returns all over again within the newer form of its replacement.

There were two powerful ideas that were underlying the euro-settler relationship with New Afrikans. Ideas that kept seeping up to the oil-slicked surface of euro-capitalist culture.

The first was that this entire continent was needed by the "white" man, and belonged to them as their God-given space.

The second is that New Afrikans are not just human beings like other people, but something very different. And

that what is so different or deviant about them is what will be responsible for their disappearance. That euro-capitalism and its settler servants have only "clean hands" about this ugly business.

The idea that this one euro-settler capitalist civilization must expand to cover the entire land mass of the continent, and even extend its power beyond, was one of the most dominant strategic political ideas in all of u.s. his-story. The popular phrase "Manifest Destiny" summed that up. We all know this already. Or should. During the Mexican-American War of 1847, the editor of the journal *Scientific American* boasted: "We hold the keys of the Atlantic on the east and the Pacific on the far distant west. Our navies sweep the Gulf of Mexico and our armies occupy the land of the ancient Aztecs… Every American must feel a glow of enthusiasm in his heart as he thinks of his country's greatness, her might and her power."

The book *Settlers* relates how "…even during the Civil War, the House of Representatives issued a report on emancipation that strongly declared: '…*the highest interests of the white race, whether Anglo-Saxon, Celt, or Scandinavian, require that the whole country should be held and occupied by these races alone.*'" That's the u.s. congress, that's "democracy" speaking.

At that same time, the peculiar idea was widespread among educated settlers that New Afrikans were not merely "inferior" to the "white" man, but so frail or unmanly as a species that they were in the process of dying away. Dwindling towards natural extinction like other failed extinct species of the past, or even the noble but "savage" Indian who somehow couldn't survive close to "civilization." Indeed, many "white" men then unfavorably compared the "wild" Indian to the Black man, whose presence on the continent was but an artificial creation of sordid business. That popular novelist James Fenimore Cooper told his readers that Nature had *"caused the African mind to wither,"* so that an Indian is *"vastly the superior of the black."*

Henry Louis Gates's 19th century predecessor as Harvard University's "expert" on New Afrikans was Louis Agassiz, an eminent scientist from Switzerland who stressed how he had no backward amerikkkan prejudices when it came to race. Agassiz was also quick to inform the public how New Afrikans were not only less manly than the euro-settler, but less of a man than indigenous peoples: "The indomitable, courageous, proud Indian, in how very different a light he stands by the side of the submissive, obsequious negro..." (To complete his kkk-grade scientific explanation, Harvard's Agassiz added, "or by the side of the tricky, cunning, and cowardly Mongolian.")

Now, Agassiz was an important voice back then, among the settler elite. Because he was one of the most distinguished naturalists and anthropologists in the u.s. He was the founder of Harvard's Museum of Comparative Zoology. Nor could he be dismissed as some right-wing nutcase. In fact, Agassiz was a liberal, and an old friend of Mikhail Bakunin, the famous Russian revolutionary. Louis Agassiz even hosted Bakunin when the controversial anarchist was making his way across the u.s. back to Europe after his celebrated escape from Czarist exile in Siberia. So it meant something when Agassiz testified before u.s. president Lincoln's Freedman's Inquiry Commission that it wasn't "safe" to let New Afrikan men vote or have the same human rights as euro-men. Human rights for women wasn't even a question, of course.

During his run-up to the presidential campaign, Abraham Lincoln echoed the popular settler view that New Afrikans were too unsuccessful a species to survive here. Slavery itself, Lincoln had declared, was also on its way to "ultimate extinction." Just like New Afrikans as a people. He said in 1857 that New Afrikans had failed to show any progress in their abilities since the time of the first British colonies over two centuries before, and that "their ultimate destiny has never appeared so hopeless as in the last three or four years." That actually was the dominant view of his entire political party.

William Seward, us. senator from NY and soon to be Lincoln's secretary of state, said in his major speech during the 1860 election campaign: "The great fact is now fully realized that the African race here is a foreign and feeble element, like the Indian incapable of assimilation..." Soon, the anti-slavery senator Seward promised his audiences, New Afrikans would join the Indians and "altogether disappear." That is, Black Genocide, in this lightly disguised form or that, was a major and popular part of "white" election campaigning. Just as it is today, in somewhat better disguise. Or didn't we notice that?

This theme was backed up, decade after decade throughout the century, by many pseudoscientific euro-settler con artists. Nathaniel Shaler, a disciple of Agassiz who became dean of the Lawrence Scientific School at Harvard University, wrote for *The Atlantic Monthly* in 1884 that New Afrikans' "animal nature" made them "unfit for an independent place in a civilized state." They were dying out, Shaler declared, and should be scattered around the country so that their terminal care should not be too much of a burden on any one area. (You can see why Malcolm X once remarked, *"Harvard has killed more niggers than alcohol."*)

One authoritative book on New Afrikans, written by Frederick Hoffman of the Prudential Life Insurance Company, and published by the American Economic Association in 1896, declared that the poor health of New Afrikans didn't come from any poverty or oppression, but from their hereditary weaknesses and natural immorality. Hoffman foresaw that these "race traits and tendencies" would weaken New Afrikans "until the births fall below the deaths, and gradual extinction results."

In some cases, this settler attempt at a pseudoscientific rationalization blamed our own Mother Nature herself.

Such as deciding that New Afrikans were really tropic beings who were biologically unable to adjust to more amerikkkan climates (unlike the strong, adaptable white man, of course). As late as the World War I period, in 1919, leading sociologist E.A. Ross wrote that the reason New Afrikans were a steadily declining percentage of the population was that *"in the North the climate does not suit them and they tend to die out."* The obvious point is that this view of Black Genocide through gradual, "natural" extinction, no matter how illogical, unfactual, or plain crackpot it was, became quite respectable among the male minds that held the steering wheel of u.s. civilization. Ross, for example, was one of the most influential liberal reformers of his age, and was later elected head of the American Sociological Association. And was chairman of the American Civil Liberties Union, on top of that.

Not only were euro-settlers active in promoting theories that New Afrikans were going to become extinct, but they insisted that any such genocide was not the responsibility of euro-capitalism. It was solely due to the alleged "natural" flaws *within* New Afrikans themselves. Perhaps the leaders in these intellectual gangs of settlers with absolutely "clean hands" were the many Anti-Slavery abolitionists who also believed that freedom meant doom for New Afrikans. Because this not too hidden desire for a pristine "white" continent was not an extremist right view, but was something both liberals and conservatives not so secretly shared. As the book *Settlers* reminded radicals:

> *Nor was it just the right-wingers that looked forward to getting rid of "The Negro Problem" (as all whites referred to it). All tendencies of the Abolitionists contained not only those who defended the human rights of Afrikans, but also those who publicly or privately agreed that Afrikans must go. Gamaliel Bailey, editor of the major abolitionist journal* National Era, *promised his white readers that after slavery was ended all Afrikans would*

leave the U.S. The North's most prominent theologian,
Rev. Horace Bushnell, wrote in 1839 that emancipation
would be "one bright spot" to console Afrikans, who were
"doomed to spin their brutish existence downward into
extinction…" That extinction, he told his followers, was
only Divine Will, and all for the good.

Rev. Theodore Parker was one of the leading spokesmen
of radical abolitionism, one who helped finance John
Brown's uprising at Harpers Ferry [Rev. Parker was the
leader of the "Secret Six", who supplied the funds and
rifles for John Brown, first in Kansas, and then for the
historic Harpers Ferry expedition – editors], and who
afterwards defended him from the pulpit. Yet, even Parker
believed in an all-white "America"; he maintained that:

"The strong replaces the weak. Thus, the white man
kills out the red man and the black man. When slavery
is abolished the African population will decline in
the United States, and die out of the South as out of
Northampton and Lexington."

Perhaps the strangest of these settler theories about Black
Genocide was the one that New Afrikans were destined to
either die out or always be "the servants of servants," because
their men were not really masculine at all, but… feminine!
This is never discussed anymore, but was one of the most
revealing sides to the entire "white" macho public discourse
on Black Genocide. To no surprise, Harvard University's
Louis Agassiz was one of the proponents of this view. Agassiz,
incidentally, as a superior euro-men's rocket scientist, reassured his public that Europeans and Afrikans didn't share
any heredity at all, but had biologically evolved completely
separately. Now, that was Segregation with a vengeance,
Jim Crowing all the way back into even Segregated fossils!
Ah, patriarchal capitalist civilization, we will miss its always

surprising entertainment value when it's gone. As we said in *Night-Vision*:

> *...Afrikans were like white women, it was said, in that their natural abilities were in the areas of intuition and emotion. This could allegedly be seen in their superiority in gospel music, religious fervor, and sexuality.*

> *The preeminent amerikkkan anthropologist of that time, Harvard's Louis Agassiz, told President Lincoln's Freedman's Inquiry Commission that he believed that it wasn't "safe" to let African men have political power, because they were in his words: "indolent, playful, sensual, imitative, subservient, good-natured, versatile, unsteady in their purpose, devoted and affectionate." Just what capitalism had ordered women to be in the dominant judeo-islamic-christian ideology.*

> *In "The Negro", his famous speech before the 1863 American Anti-slavery Convention, white abolitionist editor Theodore Tilton scoffed at prejudice against the Afrikan man just because of his different mental ability. Tilton, as a "friend" of the Negro, pointed out how unreasonable this was, since the woman-like Afrikan man could not fairly be compared to the born-to-rule, truly masculine white man:*

> **"In all those intellectual activities which take their strange quickening from their moral faculties—processes which we call instincts or intuition—the negro is the superior to the white man—equal to the white woman. The negro race is the feminine race of the world... We have need of the negro for his aesthetic faculties... We have need of the negro for his music... But let us stop questioning whether the negro is a man."**

This is a momentary flash of something much larger, what it means that genocide was rooted in gender-class.

So what was that whole thing really about? That whole mainstream discussion from presidents and preachers, scientists and economists, trade union leaders and writers, confidently predicting the complete "natural" extinction of New Afrikans from this continent. Talking about those whose labor in cotton fields, in mines and factories, in settler homes and offices, really built and paid for this entire society from skyscraper to skyscraper. How unreal and fantastical can such a political discussion be? And yet it went on within the euro-settler power structure for several centuries...

In part, it is about de-humanizing the oppressed in the process of genocide. Doesn't this always take place? Like, the Nazis, after they passed their Racial Laws, forced German Jews on their new national racial identification cards (which were cruder than the ones the Obama regime is trying to impose) to standardize their names. Jewish men had to all adopt the first name "Moses," while Jewish women had to all become "Rebecca" or "Judith." It was a petty thing to most Germans, minor perhaps in the brutal bloodbath of all that mass dislocation and killing that was happening. But it not only demonstrated the humiliating hand of the oppressor to rewrite the identity, the face, of the oppressed any way they wanted, it also worked to dehumanize Jews as alien beings who weren't like "normal" human beings. (Which just reminded me, right now, on my job sometimes the "white" middle-class male customers just call all the undocumented Mexican workers "Juan," as another way to say "Hey you, Mexican," as though they didn't each have a real name).

The Cherokee artist-activist Jimmie Durham writes about how euro-capitalism dehumanized Indians they were genociding by denying them their actual names and titles. Which are always translated into English in an out of cultural context, silly way. So we don't refer to the 1940s–50s French leader "Chief Charles the Gaul" or the great German composer "Beet Patch." We use their real names, General

Charles DeGaulle and Ludwig Beethoven. But when it comes to Indians, then it's "Chief Sitting Bull," not Tatanka Iotanka. As Durham says, it dehumanizes Indians and gives them a "not-real" and "backward" identity as nations and peoples. He points out that euro-settlers developed a special romanticized and colonial vocabulary in English just to do that as part of genocide.

The prediction of such a human cataclysm as some "natural" passing away also avoids responsibility for what are major crimes. Erecting a protective ideological framework around the oppressor. There's a reason, you know, why Adolf never signed his name to any state papers deciding his Holocaust. As the intellectuals say nowadays, what euro-capitalism was doing back then was contextualizing the discussion. i mean, while mainstream discussion of genocide here always tees off from Nazism, those Berlin guys were truly amateurs. The real pros weren't named "Heinrich," they were named "John" and "George" and "Thomas" and were always going on about "democracy." No, the real pros were right here, on this continent. Look at their batting average.

The reason so many settlers believed in the inevitability of New Afrikans being "naturally" swept aside, pushed out, or just eliminated, is that as an empire they had already done this before. To other peoples *three times* before, quite successfully. To clear most of this continent for themselves, as a special masculine people who were the chosen bearers of the euro-capitalist virus that pretends to be a civilization. Not only were the Indian nations killed off and largely relocated away West of the Mississippi, but the Mexican peoples had one-third of their territory suddenly taken. Large scale "pogroms" by settlers in Northern California cleared the territory of most Mexicans. While the Chinese Exclusion Act of 1882 removed the other half of the "colored" colonial working class that settlers used to first open up the mining, agriculture, and industry of the West Coast for them. So why not "do" New Afrikans, too, in their turn, when settler society was finished using them up?

When we read these old settler ideas today, they seem crazy. Like a prime example of what the Greeks meant by hubris–an overbearing pride and arrogance that recognizes no limits, to the point of self-destruction. But these were expressions of a confident, truly cocksure culture of victorious conquerors. A viral civilization who thought themselves collectively heirs to the gods. Which doesn't mean that their thoughts were not in some sense practical, in a serial killer kind of way.

TRANSITION TO WORLD EMPIRE

So the public idea of Black Genocide in the "American" mind had gradually evolved. First, from the early vision of open warfare, resulting in violent extermination, to the more anonymous idea of a gradual "natural" extinction. Which would be supposedly caused in the first place by the assumed deviant and subhuman nature of New Afrikans themselves. But in the early 20th century, certainly by the 1920s, this subject took another sharp turn.

While the public discussions of Black Genocide had been led by the u.s. ruling class and its servants themselves in the 18th and 19th centuries, in the 20th century it disappeared as an open question on the mainstream political surface.

Settler talk of *"sending them back to Africa"* and *"we need to help the mud races die off"* was banished to the bar and the street (where it has never diminished). And on the level of political programs, to the far right political margins. Where once the settler capitalists and their political-intellectual managers themselves were saying those things, now such proposals were marked as coming from the mouths of the far "white right." Although this settler fringe is often quite popular in terms of euro-settler public opinion.

The public position of the patriarchal capitalist ruling class and its institutions, while heavily racist, now supported the continued role of the New Afrikan colony within the u.s. empire's economy. Moreover, the u.s. ruling class continued the fake public role of benevolent "friend" and "protector" of New Afrikans. In other words, the modernized plantation ruler.

While we cannot here go into all of the reasons why euro-capitalism had to drastically change its discussion of the future amerikkka, much of it is pretty obvious. Such as the mass resistance by New Afrikans themselves. But also significant was the glaring fact that New Afrikans were rapidly growing in numbers, not declining. And the shift towards a modern industrial economy had made them even more indispensable to capitalism, not less so.

The four million New Afrikans at the time of the Civil War, had become eight million New Afrikans when Booker T. Washington became "the most famous Negro in America," at the turn into the 20th century. In 1907, New Afrikans were

New Afrikan workers at the Alexandria (Virginia) Glass Factory, 1911.

almost 40% of all steelworkers in the South, while still being
the primary agricultural workforce producing the lucrative
Southern cotton, tobacco, sugar, and rice, as well as other
crops. During the industrial boom of World War I, New
Afrikan labor was drawn North and West by the hundreds
of thousands, creating large urban "ghettoes" in the major
Northern cities. Labeling New Afrikans as "frail" and "unable to thrive," much less "dying out," became too unrealistic
to believe anymore.

And as for doing away with them, no sane capitalists
wanted that anymore back then. Euro-capitalism wanted
nothing more than to keep New Afrikans hard at work for
little wages, still the most profitable part of the u.s. economy.
Leronne Bennett, Jr. pointed out: *"Between 1870 and 1910, cotton production tripled, and the appropriated black surplus helped
pay for the reconstruction of the South, the industrialization of the
North, and the Western settlement."*

At this same time, a unity was finally acknowledged between the capitalists of the North and the South on "The
Negro Problem." While they would still use competing but
complementary systems of patriarchal capitalist control – the
nakedly violent colonial rule of "Segregation" in the South,
complemented by the outwardly more "democratic" rule by
neo-colonialism in the North – ex-Union and ex-Confeder-
ate settlers would respect and honor each other's regional
systems. The groundwork had been laid by the Hayes-Tilden
Compromise of 1877, but it was in the 1900–1920s period
that full reconciliation within the ruling class was finally
achieved on how to exploit and hold New Afrikans captive.

The raw, degenerate racial rants of South Carolina's
Pitchfork Ben Tillman, definitely embarrassed other settler
political leaders at that time. As when he openly boasted
in u.s. senate debates on how the settlers had taken down
Black Reconstruction: *"We took the government away. We stuffed
ballot boxes. We shot them. We are not ashamed of it. The Senator*

*from Wisconsin would have done the same thing. I see it in his eye…
we eliminated as I said, all of the colored people whom we could…"*
But the infamous Pitchfork Ben Tillman was so popular
among the settler electorate that his lack of subtlety was
tolerated. In truth, in his hate-filled rants in the u.s. senate, what Pitchfork Ben was really celebrating was the final
unity of settlers North and South over re-enslaving the New
Afrikan colony:

> *The brotherhood of man exists no longer because you shoot
> negroes in Illinois, when they come in competition with
> your labor, as we shoot them in South Carolina when
> they come in competition with us in the matter of elections.
> You do not love them any better than we do. You used to
> pretend that you did, but you no longer pretend it, except
> to get their votes.*

The election of Woodrow Wilson as u.s. president in 1912
marked the conclusion of that process that Pitchfork Ben
and his klansmen were so happy about. While Wilson, a
scholar and the former president of Princeton, is mostly
known today in patriarchal capitalist his-story as an advocate of "world peace" and for championing the League of
Nations, he would have been a dedicated plantation owner
of old if he could have.

Wilson's was the first u.s. administration to fully
abandon the post-Civil War era federal "Black" patronage
in Southern government and civil service. He ordered the
segregation of government employees by race, in terms of
jobs, eating and restroom facilities. Further, Post Office and
Treasury officials were given the power to retroactively "seg"
their workforces. Many New Afrikan postal workers in the
South were fired. Others demoted. In 1913 the IRS Collector
for Georgia happily declared to the public, *"There are no
Government positions for Negroes in the South. A Negro's place is
in the cornfield."*

In all this, Wilson was only mirroring the open shift in Northern ruling class opinion. An influential editorial in the *New York Times*, on May 10, 1900, admitted: "Northern men… no longer denounce the suppression of the Negro vote in the South as it used to be denounced in reconstruction days. The necessity of it under the supreme law of self-preservation is candidly recognized." Again, the ideological principle is invoked that whenever New Afrikans are struck down by settlers in any way, it is always justified as "self defense." As when the team of New York City cops a few years ago, shot an unarmed Black man *41 times…* they all said in "self defense." Case closed (a few official apologies for the mishap were sent to the family).

Even the rocket scientists at Harvard University played their reactionary role, as usual, publicly defending "Segregation" as a necessity whenever there were *too many* colored people. Berea College had always had integrated classes, but in 1907 the State of Kentucky ordered Berea to separate its students into "Jim Crow" classrooms. There was a public controversy, and Harvard president Charles W. Elliot stepped in to rally Northern support for the Southern "Jim Crow" laws:

> *Perhaps if there were as many Negroes here as there, we might think it better for them to be in separate schools. At present Harvard has about five thousand white students and about thirty of the colored race. The latter are hidden in the great mass and are not noticeable. If they were equal in numbers or in a majority, we might deem a separation necessary.*

The president of Harvard had no fear in publicly asserting one of the rules of euro-settler civilization: that a few New Afrikans here or there could be tolerated in settler civilization, but if there are "too many" of them they should be confined, forced to move on, or eliminated.

"WE CHARGE GENOCIDE"

The u.s. empire's triumphal change in world position after World War II meant that the emperor needed brand new clothes. The "American Republic" had taken hegemony over not only the Americas, but Western Europe and much of Asia, Afrika, and the Middle East as well. Washington was now the HQ for what had formerly been the separate Japanese, British, French, Belgian, Dutch, and German colonial empires in the Global South. In its new role as the center of world capitalism, the u.s. empire's strongest propaganda weapon was the myth of its "democracy" and his-story of freeing people of color. So "brotherhood" and "gradual progress" were the watchwords coming from the Big House, not colonial extermination.

But in a major counter-attack, the suppressed question of Black Genocide reappeared on the political surface once again–but now on the other side, as a radical political weapon. On December 17, 1951, a New Afrikan petition titled *"We Charge Genocide: The Crime of Government Against the Negro People,"* was presented to the world. William L. Patterson, author of the book by the same name on which the petition was based, and the executive director of the Communist Party front-group, the Civil Rights Congress, recalls presenting his petition:

> *Addressed to the United Nations it was submitted to that body in Paris, France at the Palais Chaillott where the Fifth Session of the General Assembly had gathered. Simultaneously a delegation led by Paul Robeson presented copies to the office of the Secretary General of the UN in New York. We had two aims: to expose the nature and depth of racism in the United States; and to arouse the moral conscience of progressive mankind against the inhuman treatment of black nationals by those in high political places.*

The list of those signing the petition was large and impressive. A few well-known signers:

- Paul Robeson – the great singer, actor, and once All-American football star
- Ferdinand Smith – leader of the National Maritime Union of merchant seamen
- Aubrey Grossman – the labor movement and human rights lawyer
- Rosalee McGee – the wife of Willie McGee, who was executed in 1951 after a nationally controversial trial, on the false charge of raping a euro-settler woman
- W.E.B. DuBois – the great scholar, writer and founder of the NAACP, the most prominent New Afrikan intellectual for generations
- Josephine Grayson – whose husband, Francis Grayson, was one of the Martinsville Seven, executed in Virginia on false charges after a much-publicized trial in 1951
- Ben Davis – New York City councilman from Harlem & Black CPUSA leader
- George Crockett, Jr. – Detroit civil rights leader, soon to be a distinguished judge and then a long-term u.s. congressman

The book and petition campaign, as well as the world appeal to the United Nations, was a bold move by the Communist Party USA. With some 400,000 members in 1945, as well as holding leadership positions in trade unions and civil rights struggles, the CPUSA was the most powerful left settler organization in the u.s. empire. But at that point it was crumbling under repression, from the attack by the u.s. government as the Cold War began. The "Red Scare" campaign of domestic anti-left hysteria was well under way.

The Communist Party was attempting to take advantage of the new global awareness of genocide after the Jewish

Holocaust in Europe. In fact, even the word "genocide" was brand new then. The word had been constructed by the Polish Jewish human rights lawyer, Raphael Lemkin. He was one of those obscure individuals whose life-long activity for justice can change the world. Starting in 1933 with the League of Nations, Lemkin began lobbying international bodies and the public, calling for the specific recognition and banning of the "crime of barbarism" or mass elimination. It was hearing about the Turkish genocide against the Armenian minority when he was young that had first motivated him.

In 1944, writing about Nazi crimes in the conquered areas of Europe, Lemkin first used his new term, "genocide." On December 9, 1948, The United Nations General Assembly adopted the Convention on the Prevention and Punishment of the Crime of Genocide. Specifically invoking the provisions of this convention, the *We Charge Genocide* petition stated:

> *The genocide of which we complain is as much a fact as gravity. The whole world knows of it. The proof is in every day's newspapers, in everyone's sight and hearing in these United States. In one form or another it has been practiced for more than three hundred years although never with such sinister implications for the welfare and peace of the world as at present. Its very familiarity disguises its horror. It is a crime embedded in law, so explained away by specious rationale, so hidden by talk of liberty, that even the conscience of the tender minded is sometimes dulled…*
>
> *Your petitioners will prove that the crime of which we complain is in fact genocide within the terms and meaning of the United Nations Convention providing for the prevention and punishment of this crime…*

We shall submit evidence proving "killing members of the group" in violation of Article II of the Convention. We cite killings by police, killings by incited gangs, killings at night by masked men, killings always on the basis of "race", killings by the Ku Klux Klan, that organization which is chartered by the several states as a semi-official arm of government...

Our evidence concerns the thousands of negroes who over the years have been beaten to death on chain gangs and in the back rooms of sheriff's offices, in the cells of county jails, in precinct police stations and on city streets, who have been framed and murdered by sham legal forms and by a legal bureaucracy...

Through this and other evidence we shall prove this crime of genocide is the result of a massive conspiracy, more deadly in that it is sometimes "understood" rather than expressed, a part of the mores of the ruling class often concealed by euphemisms, but always directed to oppressing the negro people... in depressed wages, in robbing millions of the vote and millions more of the land, and in countless other political and economic facts, as to reveal definitely the existence of a conspiracy backed by reactionary interests in which are meshed all the organs of the Executive, Legislative, and Judicial branches of government...

The petition concludes that "...the oppressed Negro citizens of the United States, segregated, discriminated against, and long the target of violence, suffer from genocide as the result of the consistent, conscious, unified policies of every branch of government. If the General Assembly acts as the conscience of mankind and therefore acts favorably on our petition, it will have served the cause of peace."

Despite the evident truth that these words pointed to, the United Nations of course ignored the petition. And it was "whited-out" in mainstream media. Yet, this historic campaign made a great impression. For one thing, it terrified the Southern part of the ruling class. The original UN Convention had been strongly sponsored by the u.s. empire. The Convention had to be ratified by individual member states, and a large majority soon ratified it. But not its original sponsor, the u.s.a. Because after the 1951 *We Charge Genocide* campaign went public, the Southern caucus in the u.s. senate blocked consideration of the Genocide treaty. Fearing that New Afrikans would use it to somehow get the Southern states and some of its "seg" politicians themselves put on trial at the Hague, as genocidal criminals. In the end, the u.s. senate didn't end up ratifying the Genocide treaty until almost two generations later, in 1987.

DECEMBER 17, 1951 - PAUL ROBESON PRESENTS WE CHARGE GENOCIDE BY WILLIAM PATTERSON, TO U.N. SECRETARIAT IN NEW YORK

The *We Charge Genocide* campaign changed the serious discussion of politics within the New Afrikan communities. There was a broad educational process started, in which the definition of genocide was spread. For in Article II, the UN specifically states:

> *In the present Convention, genocide means any of the following acts committed with intent to destroy, in whole or in part, a national, ethnical, racial or religious group, as such:*
>
> > *A. Killing members of the group;*
> > *B. Causing serious bodily or mental harm to members of the group;*
> > *C. Deliberately inflicting on the group conditions of life calculated to bring about its physical destruction in whole or in part;*
> > *D. Imposing measures intended to prevent births within the group;*
> > *E. Forcibly transferring children of the group to another group.*

At times in the early 1950s, under the heavy atmosphere of u.s. repression, it was hard to see that *We Charge Genocide* had caused such a widening circle of effects. But it certainly had. The start given by that 1951 campaign became very evident in the 1960s, when New Afrikan activists and writers showed familiarity with the whole discussion of genocide and the UN Convention against it. The 1951 book and its author were referred to often, during the revolutionary struggles of the 1960s. And, respectfully.

Looking back with hindsight, though, the significant weak point of *We Charge Genocide* has become more obvious. In its strenuous effort to present a convincing, overpowering case, the Communist Party painted too shallowly, with too broad a brush.

So very important points, such as the truth that the antebellum Slave System was itself an act of genocide from the beginning, were made well. Only to became just one detail out of many poured together. Obviously, if an oppressor society takes millions of kidnapped peoples, for at least two centuries, and permanently keeps them captive, deprived of their native languages and lives, to labor under the lash and the torture rack for lifetimes, as a distinct nation of helots only allowed a sub-human life–how could that not be genocide? New Afrikans can only be a people formed *by* genocide, just as "Americans" can only be a people formed by *doing* genocide on others. That's the only way it can be, factually speaking.

But when the Communist Party writers, editors, and researchers started saying that the all too familiar oppression–the unemployment, miseducation, substandard health care, mental abuse, police violence, lack of political rights, etc. – really constituted genocide, then that's like saying that Third World people's lives all around the world qualify as genocide. In an upside down way, if every injury and everything bad and being poor just become "genocide," then the word "genocide" becomes nothing. It's just a dramatic way of saying someone is oppressed. So the meaning itself gets devalued. Which is what started happening with Black Genocide.

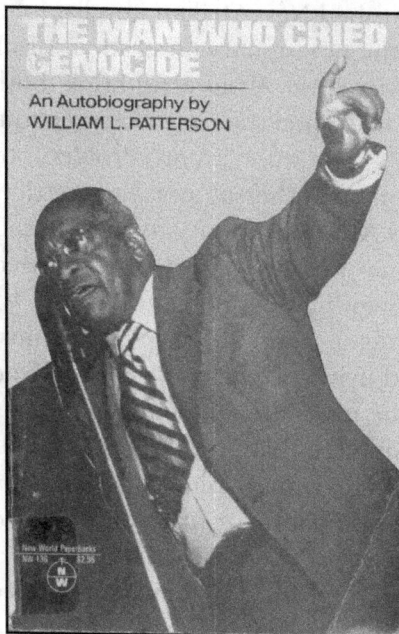

THE MAN WHO CRIED GENOCIDE

An Autobiography by WILLIAM L. PATTERSON

THE ALARM ABOUT
BLACK GENOCIDE IN THE 1960s

By that "Hot Summer" of 1967, when President Lyndon
Johnson dispatched combat-ready u.s. Army paratroopers
into the Detroit inner city to regain control, the decision for
Black Genocide had come. And genocide as a real possibility began to be discussed in the New Afrikan community.
Which even back in the 1920s ku klux klan times of segregation it hadn't. Genocide was the torn up picture that fit the
pieces coming into view. It was a community discussion not
so much polarized around an assassinated Malcolm X or an
assassinated Rev. Martin Luther King, Jr., but shaped by several influential books by Black intellectual activists. Books
that you could see people reading on buses on the way to
work, discussed on college campuses, and spread by community organizers back then.

That year the distinguished New Afrikan novelist John
A. Williams published his famous visionary novel about Black
Genocide, *The Man Who Cried I Am*. A powerful book, both
as literature and politics, it tore open the conversation about
whether settlers would really solve their "Negro Problem" by
total military extermination. Whether or not euro-settlers
read it seriously, in the New Afrikan community its battered,
well-thumbed copies became present everywhere. It turned
out that Williams was just opening the floodgates.

Williams's main character is a middle-aged jazz musician, in exile in Europe and dying of cancer. By complete accident he finds out about the u.s. national security council's
top secret "King Alfred Plan." This plan involved sealing off
the inner-city ghettoes one night with divisions of u.s. troops,
then wiping out most of the population in an all-out surprise
military assault.

As CIA assassins close in on him, Williams's unheroic
hero tries to get the word out by telephoning "the Minister"

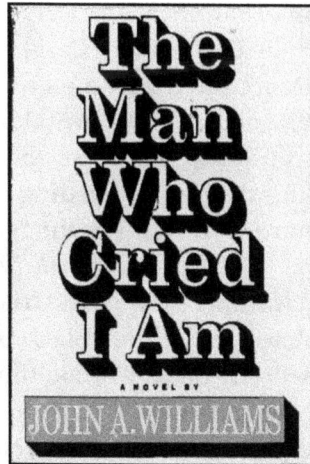

John A. Williams in 1962, five years before the publication of The Man Who Cried I Am.

(a Malcolm X-type fictional character) back in New York City. Aware that neither of them are likely to survive the onrushing firefights, "the Minister" affectionately says good-bye to the jazz musician, brother to brother: "Take some of them with you."

Now, *The Man Who Cried I Am* became a best-selling book. For a national minute Black Genocide was a popular subject. Williams's fictional "King Alfred Plan" was so realistic that it haunted people for years afterwards. Revolutionary groups like the Black Panther Party even reprinted the novel's "King Alfred Plan" text and discussed it as if it were a genuine government plan. But that *wasn't* the real strategy, as events would prove. The crisis had indeed come, but militants were already off balance, having faked themselves out of position mentally.

The next year, Sam Greenlee published his political thriller, *The Spook Who Sat By The Door.* It was an immediate

international hit. Carrying cover endorsements by come-
dian Dick Gregory and British best-selling spy novelist Len
Deighton, it became even more popular than *The Man Who
Cried I Am*. In his brutal but mocking novel, Greenlee brings
to life the fantasy of the government insider who takes his
knowledge into leading a violent revolution by the already-
hardened youth in the "gangs."

His character, the symbolically named Dan Freeman, is
a working-class New Afrikan college graduate, who is looked
down on by the "Black bourgeoisie" but who seriously and
secretly plans to wipe them out as a class. Hired as the first
Negro CIA agent in order to satisfy some racist u.s. senator's
campaign publicity, Freeman quietly spends five years at the
agency knowing that he is viewed only as window dressing.
As a Black face to "sit by the door" to make the euro-settler
CIA look a bit less racist. While outwardly accepting his sec-
ond-class role as a man who seems to humbly accept his supposed racial limitations, Freeman is really working furiously
to learn everything he can in the Agency, from martial arts
to guerrilla strategy.

When he finally feels ready for stage two in his secret
plan, Freeman quits and goes home to Chicago. Aiming at a
highly-paid position with a social work agency keeping track
of the many lumpen street organizations. As a cover, he wraps
himself in the expected consumer-crazy guise of the Black
"bourgy" who can't wait to cash in. Nice pad, Scandinavian
modern furnishings, Chev-ass Regal and Johnny Walker
Black always on the table, good suits. Like the trained agent
that he now is, Freeman blends right into patriotic "America."
Always seeming helpful to them, he becomes accepted as one
of "us" by cops and local politicians.

What no one knows, even his old girlfriend who still
tries unsuccessfully to get close to him, is that Freeman has
been doing an in-depth investigation inside the Cobras, one
of Chicago's main street "gangs." Nor do they know that

Freeman himself was once a Cobra before he saw the dead end of New Afrikan youth violently turning on each other like rats in cages. Carefully, one by one, he wins over and starts training the best Cobra leaders. From nationalist culture to guerrilla tactics. Turning what everyone still thinks is an ordinary youth "gang" into an underground revolutionary army.

Soon, youth organizations in other cities are contacted and brought in. Young underground leaders start recruiting and training an even younger generation of man-children. As Freeman reassures the police that the Cobras are no longer that dangerous, since as a "gang" they've fallen into using hard drugs more and more. When the inevitable final "riots" start, and at last the police and u.s. army are sent in to occupy and wipe out the New Afrikan communities, Freeman's underground youth army rises with deadly ambushes like a transplanted Vietcong.

Badly wounded, pinned down under fire but shooting back, having led a string of successful attacks on the invading u.s. army units, Freeman ends in a rage of rapid-fire exultation. Knowing that he has finally gotten to do what he has always wanted. Knowing that the youngest generation of child-fighters that his movement has trained is even deadlier and rapidly spreading. Freedom will be theirs.

The Spook Who Sat By The Door impressed reviewers and readers alike. It burned with a knowing rage that was not fiction. (Even though much there is naturally dated, being written when racial segregation had not yet been replaced by integration.) Greenlee was himself once a "race" pioneer in the u.s. government. At a time when Black men working for the government were usually clerks or laborers, Greenlee had been awarded the Meritorious Service Award for bravery as an officer with the u.s. Information Agency Foreign Service (a common "cover" for u.s. intelligence operatives abroad). The award was for his actions during the violent Ba'ath Party coup taking power in Baghdad, Iraq, in July 1958. It is ironic that the coup first brought into prominence an ambitious Iraqi army officer named Saddam Hussein. Greenlee had seen real armed rebellion and bloody civil war in real life. And could see it in the Black Metropolis.

The Spook Who Sat By The Door was not the first New Afrikan novel about armed revolution, but it was the first best-seller. It helped legitimize violent rebellion. It also spread the idea that the young lumpen street organizations of the 1960s were a ready-made resistance force, already brought together and armed, just waiting to be reeducated and redirected.

The questions about Black Genocide weren't confined to a few books, of course. Not only did radical groups like SNCC and the Black Panther Party raise it constantly, but even mainstream media like *Ebony* magazine (which once made it their cover story) and radio talk shows couldn't stay away from it.

In 1971, a serious nonfiction book on Black Genocide was written by Sam Yette, who at the time of its publication was a Washington correspondent for *Newsweek* magazine. A former executive with the War on Poverty, Yette was a highly respected professional journalist. This book, *The Choice*, carried a foreword by the distinguished New Afrikan writer, John Oliver Killens (the 1996 edition's foreword was by *USA Today* columnist Barbara Reynolds). Yette argues in factual detail why his people must make their choice of surviving or not, by facing the question: "Would 'Whitey' really do such a thing? Would he systematically kill off Negroes, or place them in concentration camps?"

Yette makes a plausible case for genocide much as the 1951 *We Charge Genocide* campaign did, by detailing amerik-kka's assault on New Afrikan people from all directions. From police violence to the shrinking of the numbers of farmers, and the epidemics of hunger and malnutrition. From lack of education to the readying of the old concentration camps used by the u.s. empire for Japanese-Americans during World War II.

At the center of the lethal conspiracy Yette spotlighted what he called "the Rice Cup," where old vested agricultural interests prop up high seniority Congressional white supremacists. "The five Rice Cup states are Arkansas, Louisiana, Mississippi, Texas and California... Rice Cup representatives hold the reins of power and racial prejudice here at home and profit most from wars both against racial minorities in America and rice-eating colored populations in Asia." This brave but eccentric view completely missed how capitalist power works in the u.s. empire. As though Wall Street bankers and transnational corporations weren't giving the orders.

This storm of intense New Afrikan political questioning was natural given the growing danger. But certain things marked that earlier 1960s discussion. That the pictures drawn of how Black Genocide would take place–and how to resist–were macho fantasies, which turned out to be false leads. Gradually, in a few years the spotlight on genocide dimmed. The "King Alfred Plan" scenario never happened. The sudden police roundup block by block, the all-out u.s. military assault, never materialized. Regular infantry units and national guard soldiers were sent in to regain control of the streets during the uprisings, but were soon withdrawn. People were left waiting for a thunderstorm that only rumbled in the distance.

We can see in retrospect how impossible the "King Alfred Plan" or Holocaust scenario would have been in the 1970s. For the patriarchal ruling class, it would have been like trying to cure your cancer by shooting yourself in the heart. Already up to their hips in Asian wars, how could they have risked ripping open an even bigger war right in the middle of their most valuable big city real estate? What if there were New Afrikan and Latino GI mutinies, if they even temporarily lost the u.s. capital? If they had to deal with years of urban terrorism and consumer boycotts in burnt-out major cities? And amerikkka would certainly have faced world condemnation and hatred, like Nazi Germany did or Israel should now. No, imitation Holocaust scenarios were never practical. But the unforeseen consequence of these mistaken scenarios of the 1960s was that the alarm about Black Genocide was unanswered & eventually turned off.

The other unintended side-effect of this flaw is that if genocide is what people have already experienced daily for generations, then it isn't anything new. Then, genocide isn't any new threat, any different danger. It's just same old, same old. So hearing the alert against genocide doesn't mean you have to look out for anything new. No need for an alert at all, really. This contradiction just in itself could be really dangerous, since it is disarming. So what radicals intended to have one effect, might out of unexamined political weaknesses in the long run have the exact opposite effect.

And the parable about the boy who cried "wolf!" haunts our days.

PHOTO CREDITS

26: "Policeman confronts a group at Seventh Ave. and 126th St. during renewed violence in Harlem". Library of Congress Prints and Photographs (LOC), LC-USZ62-136896. World Telegram & Sun photo by Dick De Marsico, 1964.

28: "Daniel Patrick Moynihan, head-and-shoulders portrait, speaking behind microphones, gesturing with his hands, probably at a meeting of the Senate Committee on Foreign Relations". LOC, LC-DIG-ds-01515. Photo by Marion S. Trikosko, 1976.

29: Detail, "Policeman confronts a group at Seventh Ave. and 126th St. during renewed violence in Harlem". LOC, LC-USZ62-136896. World Telegram & Sun photo by Dick De Marsico, 1964.

32: "Part of crowd in Harlem chants and taunts police on Lenox Ave. last night". LOC, LC-USZ62-136929. World Telegram & Sun photo by Stanley Wolfson, 1964.

42: "Sidewalk Merchandise On Chicago's South Side". John H. White, u.s. National Archives, 1973.

44: "Robinson, Jerry (AKA- Joseph Lewis). Inmate #22523 (MSA)". Inmate Photograph Collection, Missouri State Archives, 1920. And "Henton, Jasper O'Neil (AKA- Brown). Inmate #26153 (MSA)". Inmate Photograph Collection, Missouri State Archives, 1923.

61: "Homeless on the sidewalk." Flickr. By Franco Folini, 2008. Creative Commons Attribution-ShareAlike 2.0 Generic (CC BY-SA 2.0).

76: "Black woman with child in her lap at STFU meeting." The Kheel Center for Labor-Management Documentation and Archives, Louise Boyle, 1937.

77: "text,:) hope u can handle it!". Flickr. By Joshua Ommen, 2006. Creative Commons Attribution-ShareAlike 2.0 Generic (CC BY-SA 2.0).

81: "businesswoman". Flickr. By Erich Ferdinand, 2013. Creative Commons Attribution 2.0 Generic (CC BY 2.0).

85: "I'm proud ... my husband wants me to do my part See your U.S. Employment Service". LOC, LC-USZCN4-354. By John Newton Howitt, United States Office of War Information, 1944.

85: "Hilf auch Du mit!" LOC, LC-USZ62-59940. Theo Matejko, 1941.

88: "virginia". Flickr. Photo by Maj. Cotton Puryear, Virginia Guard Public Affairs, u.s. Army. 2008. Creative Commons Attribution 2.0 Generic (CC BY 2.0).

105: "Former slave 'Aunt Jane' with one of the J. D. Walker children". Florida State Library and Archives. Photo by G.M. Elton, circa 1885.

106: "Civil rights demonstration in front of a segregated theater: Tallahassee, Florida". Florida State Library and Archives. 1963.

112: "Shall we call home our troops? "We intend to beat the negro in the battle of life & defeat means one thing--EXTERMINATION" - Birmingham (Alabama) News". LOC, LC-USZ61-1421. 1875.

114: "Hurricane Katrina". Flickr. By Mel Silvers, 2005. Creative Commons Attribution 2.0 Generic (CC BY 2.0).

131: "Troop A, Ninth U.S. Cavalry - famous Indian fighters". LOC, LC-USZ62-76432. 1898.

141: "In the Alexandria glass factories, negroes work side by side with the white workers. Also in Richmond. These are some of those working in the Alexandria (Va.) Glass Factory. Location: Alexandria, Virginia." LOC, LC-USZ62-92162. By Lewis Wickes Hine, 1911.

149: "Paul Robeson and the Civil Rights Congress submitting We Charge Genocide petition to the United Nations Secretariat, New York, December 17, 1951,". Daily Worker/Daily World Photographs Collection, Tamiment Library, New York University.

153: "Portrait of John A. Williams, author of Night Song". LOC, LC-USZ62-113738. By Carl Van Vechten, 1962.

158: RWP (Real WorldPhoto). "A homeless black woman collects her thoughts on a curb in a parking lot."

SOME GROUNDINGS

Books women should use to teach themselves (a few of the many that Bottomfish Blues women read then that helped make this booklet's wild understanding).

Maria Mies – *Patriarchy and Accumulation on a World Scale: women in the international division of labor.*

Claudia Koonz – *Mothers in the Fatherland.* A subversive, women-centered look at not only Nazism and genocide, but its male political opponents in the liberal-left s Germany.

Toni Cade Bambara, editor – *The Black Woman: An Anthology.* This book has many voices, and is rich in the many different points of view that New Afrikan women explored coming out of the radical s.

The hidden life of today's world as revealed in women's alternative future fiction:

Octavia Butler – *Dawn.* This famous New Afrikan science-fiction writer won a McArthur "genius" award, in part for this signature work.

Suzy McKee Charnas – *Walk to the End of the World* & *Motherlines.* If men as a species wipe themselves out, how differently could women remake themselves? The second of these "horsewomen" science-fiction novels has no men in it at all.

Marion Zimmer Bradley - *Shattered Chain* & *Thendara House.* A series of fantasy novels based on a feudalistic society ruled familiarly by families of men, but the story is centered on a guild of independent women.

Since 1998 Kersplebedeb has been an important source of radical literature and agit prop materials.

The project has a non-exclusive focus on anti-patriarchal and anti-imperialist politics, framed within an anticapitalist perspective. A special priority is given to writings regarding armed struggle in the metropole, and the continuing struggles of political prisoners and prisoners of war.

The Kersplebedeb website provides downloadable activist artwork, as well as historical and contemporary writings by revolutionary thinkers from the anarchist and communist traditions.

Kersplebedeb can be contacted at:

Kersplebedeb
CP 63560
CCCP Van Horne
Montreal, Quebec
Canada
H3W 3H8

EMAIL: INFO@KERSPLEBEDEB.COM
WWW.KERSPLEBEDEB.COM   WWW.LEFTWINGBOOKS.NET

www.ingramcontent.com/pod-product-compliance
Lightning Source LLC
Chambersburg PA
CBHW072029290326
41934CB00012BA/3079